D1474729

PRINCIPAL

A PERSONAL HISTORY

CAROLINE TOMPKINS

We hope to find our work, our growth and our commitment within the institutions of our country, and in fact that is where, to some degree, we do find them—only to discover that as we do so, we are more and more extruded, or if we are not, we grow to distrust ourselves.

—James Herndon, *How to Survive in Your Native Land,* 1971[1]

All rights reserved, including the right to reproduce this book or portions thereof in any form whatsoever. For information, contact permissions@sunflowerlexical.com

Keywords: Principal, education, public schools, schools, elementary school, teacher, memoir, school reform, school administration, school leadership, democratic institutions, education policy

ISBNs: 978-0-9961581-0-7 (Soft cover)
           978-0-9961581-1-4 (e-book)

Imprint/Publisher: Sunflower Lexical
Contact: principal@sunflowerlexical.com

This book is for Mom

TABLE OF CONTENTS

NAMES AND DETAILS

THE NAMES AND PERSONAL details of many individuals, including children, parents, and teachers, have been changed to maintain the confidentiality required of a public school educator. Only one teacher, Ms. Burnett, has been composed from individual elements of several teachers at both of my schools.

Events from the more distant past are rendered as accurately as memory allows, and in some cases, following consultation with others who were involved. Where dialogue has had to be reconstructed many years after the events took place, it is faithful to the personalities and situations.

PREFACE

"FIFTY-FOUR SEEMS too young," Linda said.

She and I were sitting in her living room a few days after Christmas of the year 2000, eating tamales from plates we held on our laps. I'd known Linda longer than anyone who was not part of my family, and we hadn't had a chance yet to talk about the job—the career—I was leaving in just a few months. I had no idea how to respond.

In the years I'd worked in schools and Linda had worked as an urban planner, I'd heard her grumble about educators she saw working less than a full year, only six hours a day, and with all those long vacations. She didn't see how jobs in schools could be very hard. I didn't tell her that two principals I knew had simply cleaned out their desks and walked away on days that were not even Fridays, let alone ends of semesters. How could I tell her that after fifteen years, my job had come to feel like a game of pinball, one where I was the ball? I sat silently for almost a minute before Linda asked, "Do you think it's *futile*?"

Surprised at her use of this word, I put my fork down on my plate and said, "No! It's not futile. *I* just can't do it anymore."

Growing up in the second half of the twentieth century, I had regarded capital-P Progress as a sure thing. My postwar generation would pitch in to move America forward and by 1967, I'd decided to do my part by teaching school. I'd make sure kids could read, write, and compute, and I'd also inoculate them with peace and justice. I didn't plan on, or even imagine, being a principal.

Thirty years after I chose to teach, the era that raised me had run into trouble. Racial justice and gender equality grew, but peace did not last. Prosperity became a more elusive goal, less a value of community than a contest to be won by individuals. I didn't imagine that by the end of the last century, public education would no longer be everyone's favorite democratic institution.

In the middle of my final year on the job, an editor at a national publication encouraged me to write a thousand words about a principal's day. I began to collect artifacts and keep records. I wrote extra notes in my daily calendars, planning to show the events and conversations that any principal might face. I saw quickly that a thousand words wouldn't take me beyond the first half hour of a typical day. And each event and each conversation was only the latest knot in the tangle of threads that wound back through my entire career as a principal, my work as a researcher and teacher, and my youth as a determined schoolgirl.

As I worked to sort out the strands of my personal history as a principal, I found a complex story that demanded a more intricate structure than I had planned. In the present work, the happenings of a single day during my final spring on the job are braided with stories from my years leading two Tucson elementary schools as well as from my own life as a learner and a teacher, in and out of school.

Most of us know that there are things we don't know and, more importantly, *things we don't know that we don't know.* We might imagine that we would figure these things out during our first few years on a job. Through the years I've spent digging up and sifting the details of my life in schools, I have never stopped encountering shards of *what I didn't know I didn't know.* There is no real end to the possibilities that arise in such a search. I can only hope that the prism of memoir allows the reader to become smarter than the writer, not a bad outcome for a story such as mine.

PART 1
LEARNING
HOW TO JUGGLE

At a high school reunion a few years ago, I ran into Sandy, who'd edited the school newspaper when we were seniors. Even though we hadn't been close friends, we had always liked each other, so we sat down to trade short versions of our lives since graduation. When I told her I'd recently retired after fifteen years as a school principal, she said, "Oh! But I always thought you'd do something really important . . ." Then she blushed and changed the subject.

Chapter 1
BIRTHDAY CAKE

Today, 7:40 a.m.

I HAVE BEEN PRINCIPAL OF Brichta Elementary School in Tucson for nearly seven years, and I will retire in fifty-three days. I smooth away the remnants of a scowl, not an angry scowl, but the wrinkles that form between my eyebrows when I concentrate. Before I step out of my Honda sedan, I gather up my briefcase, lunch bag, and purse. I take a few seconds to make sure I have the three sharp-edged keys that I need to enter classrooms now that more doors are locked in the wake of the tragedy at Columbine.

Using one of the keys, I open the private entrance to my office. In this first moment, I leave the lights off and make do with the March sunlight coming through square windows on the south wall. As I open the door that leads from my office to the school's lobby, I tug at the side of my longish skirt where it has ridden up a little, and I settle on a medium smile. As I move around the corner into the secretaries' area, a tangle of children's voices hits my ears.

Three fourth-grade girls stand at the office counter, competing to be heard. Mary, our school's grandmotherly attendance clerk, stands across from them, saying, "Calm down, you all. I can't tell what you're going on about."

Like any principal, I've faced thousands of decisions about jumping into or staying out of events taking place in front of me. In the second or two I have to make up my mind, I can't always tell whether my help—the *principal's* help—is needed, or if I'm over-working my role. When my job threatens to overwhelm me and I lose track of priorities, I chance jumping into what I should delegate and handing off what should be mine. Now, if I had any sense, I would back up and let Mary tend to this.

The girls see me and one of them calls out, "Hey! Principal!"

Mary raises her eyebrows at me and retreats to her desk. I keep my smile hovering.

"What's up?" I ask.

One girl, a spindly brunette with flyaway hair, shushes the other two and announces, "The bus driver wants to see you. About Ricky. He was trying to make her crash the bus. She's really mad." She tops this off with a big grin.

If I try to avoid the bus driver, she will just stay parked at the curb until I get there, then blame me for running late on her middle school route. The girls want to be deputized, to join the posse that will haul Ricky in. I don't work that way, so I tell them, "Thanks. Thanks for your help. Go on to breakfast now. I'll take care of it." I don't move until they back away and start walking toward the cafeteria.

When I turn back to tell Susie, the office manager, that I'll be outside with the driver for a few minutes, she's picking up the phone. She looks up and signals me to wait, then tells the caller, "She's busy right now, Mrs. Bingham. Can she call you back in a little while?" Then, "OK, it'll be about 15 minutes." She looks at me to make sure I've caught this, and I nod. It's Mitchell's mom and I'll call her back when I finish hearing what Ricky's bus driver needs to tell me. I hurry out to the street.

The driver waits by the bus and I join her at the curb. She's blonde and fortyish, maybe fifteen years younger than I am. Her blue nylon jacket displays the AFSCME union logo. As if it will ensure that I'll listen, that I'll hear her, she stands closer to me than I like. I stop myself from echoing her crossed-arms stance, and I smile enough to suggest that I'm paying attention. I struggle to remember her name—Mona?

"I want him off my bus," she says.

As she spits out today's Ricky story, I work hard not to step back. I nod at what I hope are the right moments and do my best to show sympathy. When she seems to have finished, I inch backward and pronounce the principal's mantra, "OK, I'll take care of it."

I glance at her ID badge: *Myrna.*

About forty kids get on and off the bus at Ricky's apartment complex, any one of them a possible player in Ricky's daily drama. Lots of kids board the morning bus half-asleep, but Ricky does his best to wake everyone up. The driver would have to make two dangerous left turns instead of one safe right to pick up the apartment kids last instead of first, so Ricky can scout for trouble first thing.

Most days, Ricky perches on the edge of an aisle seat about a third of the way back so he can scan the new arrivals to see who has a loose edge he can work. Bus drivers hardly ever accuse Ricky of fighting or hitting anyone. They describe him as a promoter. If other kids start squabbling, Ricky jumps up and amplifies both sides of the argument until someone shoves or hits.

My calendar for today does not look crowded. It holds two teacher observations, one at 9:00 and one at 10:00, each for the required half hour. After lunch, the desegregation committee member who keeps track of Brichta is coming by to meet with me. Before she gets here, I have to look over the report I sent in a while back but do not recall in enough detail for our meeting. I also need to puzzle out how $1,200 went missing from our substitute teacher budget and see about getting it back. Before I go home today, I'll draft an agenda for tomorrow's faculty meeting and write up two teacher evaluations. Nothing out of the ordinary on this list, a medium day as these things go. To my mental calendar I now add finding Ricky and calling the mom who phoned as I was walking out the door.

Turning away from the bus curb, I cross the triangular concrete slab that covers a patch of ground between the street and the chain link that fences our schoolyard, but does not secure it. Intentional gaps remain at several points in our perimeter fence, gaps that are framed by metal poles to which gates could be attached, but are not. In front of me, a basketball bounces into the parking lot through one of these openings and a boy chases it. I start toward him, but before I call out, he grabs the ball and jumps back inside the yard. I zag back to my original path.

By longstanding custom, visitors who don't come in by the school's front door enter the playground through one of the gaps in the fence. Next, they pull open one of the eight unlocked doors to walk into the school building. No gatekeepers, no security cameras. The righteous among our visitors head to the office to obey the school district's check-in rule. But plenty of parents privilege themselves to bypass the check-in and then get snippy when one of us asks them to get a visitor badge from the office.

Not quite two years ago, a pair of high school boys in Colorado killed twelve fellow students and a teacher, wounded twenty-one others, and then killed themselves. Since then, my principal's burden of life and death sits heavier on me. As if my large urban school district has not just ordered up safety plans from all the schools, tradition welcomes the world onto our campuses. Two years after Columbine, openings in Brichta's chain link fence remain unaddressed by the centralized authority of either Buildings and Grounds or Risk Management.

Scanning the playground for Ricky, I enjoy for the thousandth time the view of the jagged natural horizon sketched by the Tucson Mountains a few miles to the west. Just south of the schoolyard fence, across a strip of new pavement, a row of stuccoed houses sits where mesquite and greasewood grew when I first arrived here. Brichta's original 1959 brick building, slightly downhill from the playground, had a classroom each for grades one through six. In the decades that followed, eight more permanent classrooms and a cafeteria were added, followed more recently by several wooden "portables" that hold four of our classes. In a more recent upgrade, the school district leveled two basketball courts and a grassy soccer field into the uneven ground just upslope from the buildings.

From the schoolyard, anyone can walk up the metal ramps and pull open the unlocked doors of the portables. Locking them against intruders would just complicate getting kids back into class after they visit the restrooms inside the school building, the only restrooms available to them. I notice again the woodpecker hole high on the east wall of Mr. McElroy's portable. Recent bee updates tell us that holes like the one on Mr. McElroy's outside wall invite the whole colony to set up camp. We are told that the bees can become fiercely territorial if we don't get them out within a month or two.

With bees, I usually get help right away from the district's safety office. But my questions about ungated entrances and free access to the portables only cause my bosses to change the subject or tell me to "figure something out." We are supposed to pretend that we're in control, that safety comes from policies and committees and plans.

Through most of my career, I've wondered if I would run toward the armed intruder, rush up the metal ramp, and shield children against a peppering of bullets. Could I obey this unwritten rule of principaling, the one that obligates me to play the hero/martyr when the need arises? I like to believe I'd cover children with my body if there is hope of saving one, but it remains an abstraction. Killer bees, pushy parents, overworked teachers, and even kids like Ricky were all on the long list of things I believed I could handle when I moved from Miller School to Brichta seven years ago.

I can *do* something about bees. I take the small yellow pad of sticky notes out of the bag where it sits with my keys and scribble Woodpecker hole. McElroy. East side above breaker box.

I scan the playground for Ricky, but when I don't find him in the next couple of minutes, I change course. Seeing him about today's bus disturbance is important, but not urgent. I pull open one of Brichta's unlocked doors and enter the hallway next to the library. Coming toward me is a third-grade boy who hugs a basketball he'd be bouncing on the tile floor if he hadn't seen me coming. As I move on, a teacher steps outside of his classroom to tell me the heating is on the blink and it's freezing in there. I tell him I'll take care of it, and I hope I'll remember this promise by the time I get back to the office.

Ricky

Even after last fall's arrival of two deeply troubled kindergartners, fourth-grader Ricky has remained my number one customer, in my office at least three times a week. Before he showed up at Brichta to join our first grade a few years ago, Ricky had bounced around in foster homes for years. By the time I met him, his mother was completely out of the picture.

When Ricky was six, his dad re-entered Ricky's life, graduated from job training, went to work in a welding shop, and found Marcia, a girlfriend of solid character. This reassembled family now rented a three-bedroom apartment in the new complex across the ravine. Still missing his mother, Ricky was adjusting cautiously to life with his dad and Marcia.

Even though he was repeating first grade, Ricky was no taller than his classmates. To further complicate his life, Ricky's face still bore remnants of a red birthmark that had once spread from his left ear into the middle of his cheek. His previous school had gotten a children's specialty hospital out of state to work at fixing this. Even though laser treatments had made the mark nearly invisible by the end of his first year at Brichta, Ricky stayed touchy about the small patches that remained.

From the beginning, just to be distracted or entertained by his blow-ups, kids poked at Ricky about his birthmark or about his missing mother. As a result, I saw Ricky a lot, which led to a comfortable familiarity between us even when he was in trouble. By the end of his first year at Brichta, I knew Ricky's home phone number by heart, something I never managed with any other student.

Ricky reached fourth grade still behind in his school work. He had trouble sitting down and paying attention, but bubbled with ideas when it was time to be creative. His powerful writing voice and colorful descriptions jumped far ahead of his spelling and punctuation. Because he was fast and agile, kids would choose Ricky for their teams, and then regret it when he changed the rules in the middle of the game. Phoning home about Ricky would usually bring his dad's girlfriend Marcia to school within half an hour.

In the early days, neither his parents nor I knew if Ricky had an attention problem or whether he was just reacting to the trauma of his early life. Ricky's dad and Marcia weren't sure kids should take drugs for attention deficits, but they went ahead and asked their doctor about it. Before the end of his first year with us, Ricky took a pill at home in the morning and another one at school. All of us, including Ricky, thought we noticed a difference. The meltdowns, bus performances, and playground brawls diminished but didn't stop entirely.

Today, 7:56 a.m.

On my way back to the office, still without Ricky, I notice a red-haired woman just ahead of me carrying a large white bakery box, the kind of box that usually holds a decorated sheet cake. I realize that she is the mother of the third-grade girl just ahead of her carrying a plastic bottle of caffeinated cola in the crook of each arm.

I stop myself from telling her that a whole cake takes too much time. Cupcakes don't require plates, forks, a spatula, extra work for the teacher, time lost from a science lesson. Cupcakes can be handed out in the last few minutes of the day. Parents, even whole families loaded down with gifts and balloons, do not always set up these classroom birthday parties ahead of time. But I lift the corners of my smile a little to hide the party-pooper attitude. I start to say, "Hi, Mrs. Go–," then realize I don't remember the last name she started using when she got married a few months ago. So I shift to, "Good Morning! Is today someone's birthday?"

I feel like I'm imitating dialogue from a poorly written movie. Here I go, with that high voice that I hate, the one with the tense undertone, a school fakery I try to avoid. The girl flashes a birthday-girl grin and reddens a little as I fuss over her turning nine. Hoping to sound more friendly than principalish, I add, "It'll help the teacher a lot if you've got a knife and spatula."

Just then, the teacher opens the classroom door and invites mother and daughter inside with a "Happy Birthday, sweetheart!"

2000, Brichta School

The year before I retired, I was working at my desk after lunch one day when the fire alarm blared. As the official overseer of fire drills, I knew I had not planned this one, that it was not our monthly practice in which Susie pulled the alarm from the office while I waited outside, timing the evacuation and checking for snags in the mass exit. I have hated the blast of the fire alarm since the red horn shrieked during my first month of first grade. As a principal, I always found a legitimate way to be outside when it went off.

That day, as I left the building and headed for the far basketball court, I had no idea what was happening. Every teacher and child, office and cafeteria worker, and a few visiting parents stood with me while fire trucks roared up to the bus curb. It took nearly an hour to establish that there was no fire, but it took us longer than that to find out that the false alarm had not been a prank.

A fifth grade class, with a couple of parents helping out, had planned an after-lunch surprise party to celebrate their teacher's birthday. Too many of the forty-something candles burned too near the smoke detector, and Ms. Kincaid didn't blow them out fast enough to keep the automatic fire alarm from emptying the building.

About an hour after that surprise explosion of sound and motion, the time wasted standing outside in the sun, the afternoon's lessons for 350 children ruined, I marched into the classroom and said in a voice loud enough for everyone in the room to hear twice over, "What on earth were you thinking with all those candles. You could have started a fire, and now look what happened, you made the whole school go outside and miss class for over an hour." The kids and adults in the room just sat there, wide-eyed.

Chapter 2

Real School

Tucson, a long time ago

AFTER MY FATHER CAME HOME to Illinois from World War II, my parents packed up their belongings and boarded a train bound for Tucson, Arizona. Here they made their home and started a family. Like most other post-war migrants to Arizona from the American Midwest, my parents had no idea they were settling in territory that the United States had purchased from Mexico less than a century earlier.

My mother fell in love with Mexican food, Mexican architecture, and Mexican-inspired home décor. She probably met a few people of Mexican heritage. She wouldn't have distinguished the newer arrivals in this purchased strip of America from those whose ancestors had settled the Mexican *Presidio de Tucson* and who had been the original social elite when the Gadsden Purchase had turned them into U.S. citizens.

I arrived about a century after the Purchase, when Tucson's population was just passing sixty thousand, and I remained ignorant of my hometown's history until I came back after graduate school to work in the schools. Only then did I find out that, generations before the 1854 purchase, Tucson's Mexican-descended families had settled along the river known as the Santa Cruz. Both before and after the international boundary was marked, the river's now-dry channel served as a corridor for traders, missionaries, refugees, settlers, farmers, criminals, and the curious.

By the 1940s, downtown Tucson had expanded a small distance beyond the original *Presidio,* while the greater city and its schools had spread east, north, and south. Even with its university and the railroad that passed through on the way from Los Angeles to New Orleans, my hometown would remain, at least until the 1950s, the middle of nowhere.

I lived my 1950s in a state of post-World War II relaxation and relative simplicity. We had won, our dads had gone to college on the GI Bill and had gone to work in offices, and our moms stayed home and joined the garden club. For my post-war middle class, things were *tidy,* a word that would hardly apply one decade later and a word that I have never felt comfortable using. My mother tells me that on the morning in 1953 when I started first grade, I stood up on my bed and hollered, "My day has came!"

Even though the neighborhood kids let me be the teacher when we played school, I couldn't wait for this pretend phase to be over. I felt sure that the red brick building at the end of our block—Cragin Elementary School—would be much more thrilling than setting up mismatched chairs in our carport for the four or five kids I could round up.

Today, 7:59 a.m.
I make it back to the office a few seconds before the 8:00 class bell. Susie smiles and says, "I've got Mitchell's mom on hold."

Mitchell comes from one of the small number of African-American families who live in the Brichta neighborhood. His parents are divorced and share custody, but mostly I deal with Mitchell's mother. I call her every month or so about Mitchell, but she hardly ever calls me. Most of the time when I phone her, she talks as if she's on my side, but not always. Sometimes she worries that I don't deal with the kids who push Mitchell to boil over, the ones who've caught on to how little it takes get him going.

As many times as I've practiced the conversation, I've never trusted myself, white and middle class, to get it right. She hasn't come right out and called me a racist, but I sense unease in the pauses between her words and sentences, the way she says, "Well, then . . ." and the way she sighs. My Midwestern Protestant parents did their best to raise me without prejudice based on color, but I took my family's abundance of opportunity for granted and grew up oblivious to the built-in privilege of my whiteness.

On this Tuesday in March, I move into my office to pick up the phone. As I have taught myself to do, I listen all the way through his mother's account of who threatens to do what to Mitchell. She says, "Caleb's saying he's going to kick Mitchell's butt after school. He's scared." As she goes on, I listen for what she means: If you call me every time my child screws up, I'm going to call you when somebody goes after him.

Not for the first time, Mitchell has turned his mother's attention to something he hasn't reported to anyone at school. Once she finishes, I stop myself from reminding her that Mitchell is supposed to tell me right away if someone threatens him so that I can investigate. I don't want a bad situation to get worse before I can do something about it. In our last meeting, Mitchell's mom sat beside me and nodded when I insisted that Mitchell give me a chance to get ahold of things right away, not to let them hang over until the end of the school day. Maybe she agreed with me just to finish the conversation, just to escape from the principal's office.

Before we hang up, she says to call her after I find out what's going on, and I promise to take care of it. Every day

I act as if I have enough control over the tumult of school that this promise holds more weight than air. If I could really fix, figure out, take care of everything, I wouldn't still be at it with Mitchell and Ricky in early March. I will only be taking care of it for today, for this week, but not guaranteeing any fix for the future.

1953

When the time came for me to start first grade, I lived with my mother and father and my little brother Tom in the cramped two-bedroom house where we had moved when Tom was a baby. My mom stayed home to take care of my brother and me, while my father was in his second or third year of working as a YMCA executive. Mom made us rabbit-shaped pancakes for breakfast and filled our yard with snapdragons, petunias, and hollyhocks. A talented artist, she sometimes earned extra money by hand-painting neckties for local shops.

At Cragin, *real* school, I would have my first *real* teacher. A month or two in a church kindergarten with a sour teacher had not spoiled my appetite for this. My fingers itched to mark on the blackboards with the white sticks of chalk and to scrub away words and numbers with the felt erasers. I longed to be the helper who'd pass out the crayons, scissors, pencils, and glue that waited in the row of cupboards near the classroom door. Best of all, books and more books lined the wooden cases under the tall windows looking out to the courtyard.

On that first *real* day, I put on a yellow chintz dress that Mom had sewn and hand-painted with circus clowns. After Mom pigtailed my hair and buttoned up the back of the dress, I managed the white socks and brown Mary Janes by myself. With Mom holding my little brother's hand, the three of us walked down our street toward the crosswalk that led to Cragin Elementary. I skipped on ahead a few times and waited for them at the end of the long block, impatient to cross the big street. When the sixth-grade boy in his white safety-patrol belt whistled traffic to a stop and raised his pole to the "go" position, I waved at Mom and waded into the surge of kids. We'd practiced this part of starting school.

I followed the other kids to the far side of the building, but when I reached the door where I was supposed to line up, enormous third graders shouted and ran around, blocking my way. I pressed myself against the wall by the door until Mrs. Aldrich came out and prodded her class—*my* class—into two lines, one for boys and one for girls, and led us like ducklings into our room.

I can't guess how old Mrs. Aldrich would have been that year. Her hair was still dark, flecked with silver, braided and wrapped around her head. The hairstyle, along with her brown calico shirtwaist, suggested "prim," but I didn't know that word yet, so to me she was just my teacher. That first morning, she told us, "Boys and girls, find your name card on the table and sit straight and tall like ladies and gentlemen."

I promptly sat by the card that said CAROLINE and scooted the chair in until my chest touched the table. I didn't notice whether the other children found their seats easily or required help. In those days, before kindergarten was part of all elementary schools, some first graders would have arrived at school not recognizing the letters of their names, but I would not have realized this at the time.

Once the twenty-three of us had made ourselves "straight and tall," Mrs. Aldrich said she would read our first names from a list and, when we heard our name, we should say, "Present." A few names in, when she got to my friend Billy, she announced that because there were two Billys in the class, he would need to be called William, while the other boy could still be Billy. It seemed normal that the teacher should make and announce decisions like this. By the time Mrs. Aldrich pronounced *"Carolyn,"* most of the other children had had a chance to say "Present." When no one claimed this name, Carolyn, I looked around to see who might be daydreaming.

Mrs. Aldrich stepped toward me and pointed at the name card taped to the table in front of me. Raising her voice a little, she said, "*Carolyn*. Carolyn *Tompkins*." I looked down at the card and it still said "CAROLINE."

Startled, I said "*Caro-LINE*." I had been paying attention, but she had not said my name.

I don't know if I ever said "Present." Mrs. Aldrich called out the last two or three names and moved on to deliver the Rules of First Grade. Not wanting to miss out on any of these, I sustained my forward lean in the chair. Each time Mrs. Aldrich called me "Carolyn," I said "Caro-*line*." She ignored me every time.

We had a full hour off at lunchtime so the kids who lived nearby could walk home to be fed by our own mothers while the other kids ate in the cafeteria. With home only a block away, my mom could hear about my morning while I ate. I was impatient to tell her that my teacher, this *real* teacher in whom I'd invested so much hope, wouldn't say my name right. "It's only the first day," Mom said. "You can try again this afternoon."

Even at six, I was in love with facts and was accustomed to winning contests of correct and incorrect. I had been reading the 1949 edition of *The Book of Knowledge*, all 20 volumes, for over a year. I especially loved the article in Volume Seven about the duck-billed platypus. Mom encouraged my hunger for information and didn't think to tell me that it might be wrong to set the teacher straight.

Today, 8:10 a.m.

As I open Ricky's classroom door, I find the kids on their feet to recite the Pledge of Allegiance. I place my right hand over my heart and say it along with them. These kids will never know about my early years of teaching, when I refused to lead my first graders in the pledge for one whole year. I was in my early 20s, the Vietnam War had only reached the beginning of the end, and I felt that this small act put me across a line from Richard Nixon.

While his classmates face the flag and mumble the pledge in rough unison, Ricky glances over at me. I watch him work his right hand from his chest up to his throat and pretend-strangle himself. As soon as they finish the pledge and the silent moment, I look squarely at Ricky and jerk my head in the direction of the office. He does a little dance of "Who, me?" before he gives in and jumps into the hallway just ahead of me.

"Hey, Ricky, how come you didn't come by to see me this morning?"

"Well, I was on my way, and I was almost there, and that teacher, I forget his name, told me 'Get outside right now.'"

As we walk toward my office, I half-listen as Ricky tries to convince me that not coming to see me was his only option. And in a funny, backwards way, he's right. Why would the teacher who told him to go outside know that—just this once—Ricky was actually supposed to be going inside?

When we're almost at my office doorway, I interrupt him.

"What's with you and the bus driver?" I start. "She says you were really impossible this morning."

"But that kid, Anthony, the one who always talks about that other kid's mom, they said that kid was going to get Anthony at lunch . . ."

Ricky goes on to show-and-tell why, today, he had to get out of his seat on the bus to take on Anthony's business. Just like everyone else, he knows that standing up on a moving school bus is strictly prohibited. He can recite the reasons for this as if he wrote the rules himself. Even so, he always passionately defends each particular decision to stand up. Ricky is impulsive and wily, with a nose for trouble and for drama, but he is not hardened. At some point, our meetings started to feel like an endless series of chess games between quarrelsome long-time friends. So this is a relationship and not merely a bust.

After a minute or two of feeling I'm trying to catch a bee in a butterfly net, I tell Ricky to stop talking and listen for a minute. I give him the usual blah-blah-blah about standing up and yelling on the bus, and tell him that today he will report to the counselor for after-lunch detention.

Since Ricky arrived at Brichta, the drivers on his route, one driver after another, have gotten fed up enough to hand me lots of the half-page "bus ticket" sheets or, as today, to invite me to the curb to hear them out. After the third complaint in a semester, I suspend Ricky from the bus for a few days. Kicking him off the bus only tempts him into other dangerous acts, like running through the desert ravine that separates the apartments from Brichta. Dotted with cactus and strewn with rocks and risking an occasional rattlesnake, the walk through this deep arroyo only takes ten or fifteen minutes, nearly a half hour less than walking the long way.

Whenever I suspend Ricky from the bus, his dad and stepmom instruct him to stay out of the ravine, to walk *around*, a route that involves two busy streets but no dangerous crossings. From the time Ricky was in second grade, this directive has not stopped him from taking the shortcut. To make it worse, he usually goes first to the bus stop near his apartment and recruits other kids to run the ravine with him, beating the bus by at least ten minutes.

If I catch Ricky at this, I call home and remind whoever answers that the shortcut is not safe. If I find out which kids went along with Ricky, I phone their parents, too. Even though I tell all of them that I can't be responsible for problems with their shortcut, I know that law and court decisions make unsafe walking to school my problem too. Just about the time I started principaling, responsibility for a child's overall welfare shifted notably in the direction of the school. We could be held responsible for so much more than we had a prayer of controlling.

Pushing to finish up, I make sure Ricky is looking at my face and I say, "I'd like you to think about what you're going to say to Myrna next time you see her."

Ricky is fiddling with the papers on my table. He wags his head back and forth and mutters "Sor-ry" in a high-pitched phony voice.

Instead of pressing an apology of doubtful sincerity, I change the subject. "Any chance you forgot your pill this morning?"

Mr. Drama hits the heel of one hand against his forehead, and says "Oh, yeah! I was gonna take it but my brother made me run for the bus."

Despite media-fueled myths about schools pushing pills on children, we have no more power to prescribe medications than to perform surgery. We do not tell every parent with a rowdy child to put him on drugs. But when I see a bright enough kid struggling to keep up in class and pulling senseless social stunts so often that no one wants to be his friend, I sometimes suggest a medical check-up. And I only do that after the teacher and I exhaust our own repertoire of ideas to engage and motivate an over-active child. Today, I don't want to hear the rest of Ricky's why-I-missed-my-pill, so I stand up and say, "Follow me. You need to say hi to Karen."

With my hands hovering above his shoulders, I march Ricky around the front counter and into the health office. The mismatched plastic chairs and the two pink vinyl cots are momentarily free of other children. Sitting at her desk across the room from the door, Karen, the health assistant, looks up and greets Ricky with an enthusiastic "Hello there!"

I ask Karen to get ahold of Ricky's dad or stepmom to see if it's OK to give him a pill from his supply that stays in our locked medicine cupboard. Karen smiles and says, "Sure. No biggie." Thank goodness, I think, for office staff who are usually nicer than I am. I stand behind Ricky and grip his shoulders just enough to keep him facing Karen, but not hard enough to suggest that he's in custody. Karen can see my face, but Ricky can't.

"Can you handle a visitor for a while?" I ask. Karen catches that I mean "until he swallows his meds and they start working."

CHAPTER 3
DUE PROCESS

Today, 8:24 a.m.

I NEED TO SEE MITCHELL about his mother's phone call, to get an idea of who might be threatening him and if it's serious. When I get to the classroom, Mitchell's teacher is explaining today's math, but stops mid-sentence as I enter. The kids who've been paying attention to the lesson now swivel their heads in my direction.

"I need to take Mitchell," I say fast, wanting to get away so the teacher can continue.

Mitchell's face brightens when I say his name. He stands up and juts his jaw to show he's not afraid of the principal. As we walk toward the office, he looks at my face to check for sympathy or alarm or any other clues about how he should pitch his story, but I have already flattened

my expression. I resist the urge to puncture his balloon
of self-importance and we stay quiet all the way back to
my office. As we pass from the older part of the building
into the new office wing, Mitchell kangaroos up to slap
his palm against the top of the doorframe. I can still be
startled by these sudden boy-moves, and I step aside to
avoid his return to earth.

He usually seems eager to tell me who is going to do
what to him, but when I start probing, Mitchell's stories
often evaporate. No other kid has ever acted on threats
against Mitchell. Even if he concocts these tales of vic-
timhood to catch his mother's attention at the tired end
of her workday, I must consider each new account as if
we haven't been there before. I can't risk Mitchell getting hurt because I disregard the at-long-last-true story
of impending harm.

As we sit down at my table, I grab my pen and notepad.
I write the date at the top of the page and say, "What's
happening with you and Caleb?" and write *"Wh hpng w/
y and C?"* in my personal shorthand.

"He's always bothering me." Mitchell says in a borderline whine.

"What's he doing?" I ask.

"He keeps saying he's gonna kick my ass after school."
He takes a quick look at my face to see if I'm reacting to
"ass," but I learned a long time ago to let this one go by if
it's just the two of us in my office.

We go on like this for a while, and I discover that two other boys, a girl in his class, someone else's little sister, and the inevitable Ricky play supporting roles. Mitchell tries to sidetrack me with an unrelated story about Ricky's brother, but I push the conversation back to center. Once I have my witness list, I press Mitchell again for when this started.

"What makes your mom think this has been going on for a long time?"

Mitchell shrugs and mumbles, "I d'know."

Partially busted, he grins for an instant and then goes poker-face again. He remembers that if all this really happened, he was supposed to come to me first.

"OK, I'll talk to some of the other kids and see what's going on. I don't want you to get your butt kicked at the apartments *or* at school."

Like the other kids, he is not sure the principal should say the word "butt," and I'm not sure myself, but I say it anyway. "Bottom" or "behind" would be too prissy and "ass" would go too far.

Today, someone or something has Mitchell, and Mitchell's mom, worked up. I won't jump to a conclusion based on my instincts or on Mitchell's history. Not exactly the mythical principal who lives to hand out punishments, I'll play detective, prosecutor, defense attorney, and, in the end, judge. I have only been on campus for forty-five minutes, and I'm already looking at the three towers of

Lawsuit City: safety and order, due process, and racial fairness. I suspect that school boards and superintendents fear being sued just a bit more than they care about low test scores.

Two years before Mitchell enrolled at Brichta, a boy named Caleb arrived in the custody of a great aunt. At first, Caleb played with Ricky at school and in each other's neighboring apartments, and the two families remained on good terms. Caleb's fervently religious aunt worked hard to nurture good citizenship and good scholarship in Caleb and his sister.

In second and third grade, before Mitchell showed up, Ricky and Caleb attracted overlapping groups of friends, with no clear division into cliques. Both of them loved attention, and neither one feared a trip to the principal's office.

As time passed, their friendship veered off into rivalry and back again, but never stabilized. When they were at odds, games could get messy fast. By the end of their third grade year, I could not predict whether they would come to school in a raging dispute or as best pals.

Last August, about the time Caleb and Ricky started fourth grade, Caleb's great aunt found out she had cancer. Facing months of treatment, she sent Caleb and his sister to relatives out of town and we didn't know if we'd see them again. Not long after Caleb went away, Mitchell moved into the neighborhood, and we put him into the class Caleb had left. A little taller than Caleb, Mitchell quickly filled in as leader of Caleb's loose-knit group, a mix of Anglo and Latino boys. I have watched the swirl of the grouping and re-grouping around Ricky, and then Mitchell, but I haven't seen rigid antagonism or drawn-out feuds, nor have I noticed any racializing of the kids' alliances or differences.

Then, about a month ago, Caleb came back. The fourth grade machos would have been happy to welcome him back into the group. But Caleb, not satisfied to share the top job with Mitchell, has been rough and aggressive on the playground. He has also put together a series of events featuring swagger, dares, and implied threats. These gatherings are heavy with the possibility of fighting, but usually stop short of any actual shoving or hitting. This posturing is not a clear violation of anything, and I am—so far—giving them a chance to work things out among themselves.

Lots of children besides Ricky and Mitchell and Caleb do not let me forget that my first duty as principal is to maintain order and safety. Only secondly do I perform the role I came for, to guide teachers to teach and children to learn. But third, the obligation that remains less evident, are the hours spent each week deeply immersed in the labyrinth of federal and state law, court decisions, and local school board policies.

For every hundred threats of "taking this to my attorney," only one might ever turn into something. Even with that statistic on my side, eventual outcomes are not always obvious at the beginning. Careful investigation gives me my best chance to figure out who provoked, who hit or pushed first, who reacted, who overreacted, who egged on, who piled on.

Miller School, 1987

I have been a devout note-taker and a careful investigator ever since Angela Pierce's father came to see me during my second year at Miller, nearly fourteen years ago. Arriving at school that morning, I walked into the front office to find my secretary, Frances, facing a tall man across the reception counter. Frances had a good business voice, warm without being breezy, but in that moment her voice came out an octave higher than usual: "Mr. Pierce is hoping to see you for a minute about Angela." The man kept his arms crossed as he turned to face me.

The day before that, a fifth-grade teacher had sent me a note saying that Angela and two other girls had threatened to beat up a classmate. The teacher who'd sent the note never asked for help unless she really needed it. She always treated kids fairly, and I trusted her to have her facts straight. I called the three suspected bullies to my office without first asking the alleged victim to tell me her side of the story. The minute the girls arrived in my office, I started in on them, "How could you . . . you all know better . . .

three against one. It sounds like you were acting like a bunch of thugs . . . I can't imagine any excuse for ganging up on her."

When I sentenced them to lunch detention and sent them back to class, two of them acted ashamed and said they were sorry. The third girl, Angela, gave me that "You don't know anything" look, the one that ripens in adolescence. I knew I should have called the parents of the two for whom this was a second offense, but I didn't call home on any of the girls that day. I rationalized that the scene in my office was a warning and that I would call parents if something else happened. It was pure luck that they didn't try any payback on the girl who told their teacher.

Now, the morning after I let loose on the girls, Mr. Pierce stood between me and my office door, with jaw muscles working and the same wanting-to-spit expression I'd seen on his daughter's face the day before. Without looking at him or at Frances, I said, "I'll need a minute to put my things down and then I can see Mr. Pierce in my office." I probably sounded as squeaky as Frances had.

I slipped past him, rounded the corner into my office, hit the light switch and dropped my purse and briefcase on the desk. By the time I turned around, Mr. Pierce was standing in the middle of the room. I slid into one of the molded plastic chairs at the round table. "Please—sit down," I said.

He stayed on his feet. "I have a few things to say to you and I don't need to sit down to say them."

I stood right back up and put myself as far around the table from him as I could.

"My daughter tells me you called her a thug yesterday. She says you yelled at her and didn't let her say anything."

I jumped to clarify. "I didn't call them thugs. I said they were *acting like* thugs."

"I believe what she told me. You called her a thug."

Caught in the wrong, I could have either slugged it out or folded, but I didn't quite get it yet. I clung to my scholar's inclination to quibble over a word or two. But I could not deny telling the girls that only thugs would gang up to threaten a classmate.

Furious at myself and at him, I managed to say, "I'm sorry I was so hard on the girls."

"I don't care about any other girls. It's *my* girl you aren't ever going to talk to like that again."

Today, 8:36 a.m.

I pull open the door of Mr. McElroy's portable and find him sitting at his desk turning the pages of a cycling magazine. His twenty-four students slump this way and that in their chairs, reading to themselves. Mr. McElroy started teaching back when I did, when it was customary to give kids time each day to read something of their own choosing. A chalk-written agenda for the day fills an end of one of the green boards. 8:30—Sustained Silent Reading tells me what they are doing now, while 10:00—Social Studies—Arizona Maps reminds me that I'll be back later to observe a lesson.

Pleased that only a few kids look up from their reading, I slip out the door and step into the next portable for just a minute. There I find children donning paper hats in preparation for acting out a scene from the American Revolution. One child is George Washington and another is General Cornwallis, each surrounded by a team of Patriots or Redcoats.

No principal has the luxury of spending the day working with one kid at a time. Today, just like every day, I must figure out how to visit classrooms, all the classrooms. I need to show up when teachers and kids expect me *and* when they don't. Even in my lame-duck year, I have no intention of making fewer visits to the classes. The school district complicates this part of my job with the satisfaction survey they send out to parents, kids and teachers every January. One item says, "The Principal visits my classroom every day."

When I visit their rooms three or four times a week, the kids stop noticing me. I might as well be invisible, which is fine with me. The kids' job is to pay attention to their teachers and do their work. In educator jargon, this is "student engaged time," or "uninterrupted learning time." Should I clatter into their rooms once a day so they'll register my visit and give me higher ratings on the survey? Would I need to do this all year, or just during the month or two before the form goes home? Most of the time, I choose stealth, but I might have staged a few grand entrances in the first weeks of January.

Over the years, on average, I've managed to visit each classroom about three times a week. Some days I just step inside the door for a minute or less, and on other days I stay long enough to see what's being taught and learned. How long would I need to stay to see what's really happening? When life is too busy, I check off the rooms where I pick up kids for interviews and investigations even if that is all I do there.

I hurry up the metal ramp of Ms. Langer's portable, the one that holds the fourth- and fifth-grade special needs class, and remember to slow down and open the door gently. I don't want to act as if I'm hot on someone's trail. Inside, a few of the kids lounge on a sofa, reading with their teacher, while others work at tables with papers and books. The two kids I was worried about seem to be OK—in fact, Dino snuggles against his teacher's shoulder, but it's only the first hour of the school day.

Sitting in another part of the room next to one of the computers is a thin boy named Brian, whose dark brown hair hangs low over his eyebrows. He's wearing the glazed look he gets on the days no one is home to send him off to school. His mother's swing-shift job at the reservation casino probably turns into an all-nighter more than we can know. Like one other boy in the class, Brian has a diagnosis of bipolar illness, identified when an emergency medical clinic sent him to the hospital for a few days after some kind of ruckus at home. He seems to get his medicine on some days but not on others.

Brian's body stiffens. Without turning his head to look straight at me, he gives me a slit-eyed sideways look I've seen before. I shift my attention away from him just as the teacher looks up and says in a soft voice, "Brian, what are you doing?"

"Nothing!" he screeches. His arm swings out and a pile of loose papers sails to the floor around the computer desk. Hoping that he might feel less inclined to perform if I'm not in the room, I back up and turn to the door.

Just as I didn't have at Miller, I have no control over what special needs classes or children central office sends me. The district calls this class "cross-categorical." It mixes children branded learning disabled, mildly mentally handicapped, and "other health impaired," a mysterious label with no clear edges. Brichta's cross-categorical class pulls in a dozen kids from all over the western half of our very large district.

On my way out, I pass the teaching assistant, a kind woman who was working at Brichta when I arrived. Waiting at the bottom of the ramp for me to complete my exit, she carries a sheaf of papers in one hand and in the other balances a full mug of coffee. I bite my tongue about the coffee. Looking back, my no-coffee-in-the-classrooms directive seems old-fashioned, even mean-spirited, considering what people may need as they face a school day. I can't even remember if the rule was my attempt to save the raggedy classroom carpets or if I'd adopted it from a principal before me.

Checking to make sure that no child is poking a head out the door to listen, I tell the aide that Brian is wound up and might need to see the counselor. She smiles with sad eyes and just says, "OK." We both know that a trip to the counselor's office might calm Brian down a little, but won't make his troubles go away.

CHAPTER 4
RACE AND PRIVILEGE IN THE BORDERLANDS

The 1950s, Tucson

IN THE SUMMER OF 1954, just after I finished first grade, my dad opened America's first family YMCA in a two-story adobe house that someone had donated for this purpose. We would actually live at this YMCA, my parents said, and I would go to second grade at a new school. By Labor Day, we had squeezed our family of four into a tiny two-bedroom apartment that sat behind the main house.

Jake, the janitor for this YMCA branch, moved with his wife Beatrice into an apartment even smaller than ours, one that faced an alley at the back of the property. Mom explained that while our apartment had been a guest house, Jake's apartment had once been servants' quarters, something I'd never heard of. She made it clear that Jake and Beatrice were *not* servants even though they were *Negroes*, a polite term in the language of that era, a term that fell out of use a decade or so later.

African-Americans made up—as they still do—a slim percentage of Tucson's population. Until the 1950s, one school near downtown served almost all of Tucson's black children in grades one through nine. That school was closed a year or so before the Supreme Court decision that mandated racial integration, and the children were relocated to formerly all-white schools. Even so, the segregation of neighborhoods ensured that African-American children would remain largely clustered in just a couple of schools, in *de facto* segregation, well into the 1970s.

When I was in second or third grade, my mother observed that some Mexican families named their sons *Jesús*, which she pronounced *Jee-zus*. Oblivious, even here in the borderlands, my parents assumed that we, the European-descended immigrants from the Midwest, were the norm. We were the standard-issue Americans in a region that would increasingly *otherize* the fourth and sixth generations of Ochoas or Carrillos in this purchased territory. By the time I came back to Tucson from getting my master's degree in 1970, *Mexican-American, Hispanic, Latino,* and *Chicano* competed with each other in the language of reference and of identity.

After we moved to the new YMCA in the adobe mansion in 1954, I walked the four blocks to second grade at my new school. I made friends quickly enough that my teacher detained me more than once to write twenty-five lines of "I will not talk." One of the other kids showed me how to write "I" twenty-five times down the page, then "will," and so on, to give some vertical variety to the task.

By mid-autumn of the next year, my third-grade teacher scolded me for trying to use math flashcards reserved for second semester. I began taking off my shoes and sitting on the floor next to my desk. This way, my teacher couldn't see me from behind her desk or even from her usual spot by the blackboard at the front of the room. Later my mother told me that the teacher had told the principal she thought I might be retarded.

This resulted in a four-year detour in a small private school that advanced me a grade level and gave me a scholarship. When I returned to the public schools for ninth grade in my neighborhood high school, there were over 600 kids in my freshman class. Bored in English by a teacher trained to teach biology, I once again got in trouble for talking too much. By my second year,

I started noticing how school seemed to mimic real life without *being* very real. We studied *about* things without actually doing much.

During my early years of high school, Tucson's city council passed an ordinance forbidding racial discrimination in public accommodations. Along with my church youth group, I got ready to paint signs and march in front of a local diner that openly defied the law. A little later, our pastor had us read Martin Luther King's "Letter from Birmingham Jail," and he strummed "We Shall Overcome" on his guitar.

Real life, or at least a version of it that made sense to me, had begun showing up, but not in school. During the summer before I started my senior year, my mom and I watched on TV as Dr. King stood in front of the Lincoln Memorial and declared his dream. With my liberal passion now focused on the civil and human rights of African-Americans, I remained as ignorant of my city's Hispanic heritage as my mother had been when she stepped off that train from Illinois.

In the late fall of senior year, during a quiz in my journalism class, the other kids and I heard over the loudspeaker that President Kennedy had been shot in Dallas. The teacher collected our half-finished papers and sat with her head in her hands until the bell rang. Next period, we sat in front of a TV in American Government class and watched as bad news got worse.

In the winter, I helped circulate my first protest petition when a girl I knew was banned from the honor society for wearing culottes to school. I skipped the mandatory baccalaureate before my June graduation, explaining this in a letter to the principal as if he hadn't heard of the First Amendment. It's possible that he hadn't, since he was the same principal who had tried to ban a harmless student humor magazine two years earlier.

Today, 8:48 a.m.

Up another metal ramp in search of my Student Council president, I tug at the doorknob of the fifth grade portable. The door is locked and the room empty. Earlier this morning, in my wire basket, I found a note penciled on blue-lined school newsprint.

> Dear Dr. Tompkins,
>
> We would like to make an appointment to talk to you about some Student Council business.
>
> Sincerely,
>
> Alicia and Daniel

On the outside wall next to the door, Alicia's teacher has hung a paper plate marked into five or six labeled pie slices that indicate the various possibilities: Library, Playground,

Computers, etc. A plastic-laminated cardboard arrow that rotates from the center tells me that the class is at lunch, but it's not even 9 o'clock in the morning. Clomping back down the ramp and out to the rear of the portable, I find the class scrambling around the basketball court, throwing inflated red rubber balls at each other. Their teacher is the one whose birthday candles set off the fire alarm last year. It had taken me a week to crawl back into her classroom to apologize.

In that last-name way we school people often use in front of children, I say, "Hi, Ms. Kincaid. How's it going?"

"So-so. OK, I guess."

Three surgeries for back trouble have not brought back the agility that Ms. Kincaid needs to keep up with fifth graders, even the small class of twenty she has this year. Neither of us really knows what to do about this. I worry that she could lose some of what I call her "preacher voice," the one that for years has urged and inspired her classes to outdo themselves, and later to write her into their essays about "The Best Teacher I Ever Had." The pain eats at her, stealing her energy for this hard work. She stays courteous and professional with me whether I deserve it or not. I can't help but wonder, each time I see her, if she has forgiven me.

Now Ms. Kincaid calls Alicia out of the game, and the girl and I retreat from the noise. One of the nearly sixty percent of our students who count in our census as Hispanic, Latino, or Mexican-American, Alicia is tall and dark-haired, a third-generation American. Her mom manages a restaurant and her dad is a software engineer. Alicia responds to my "How are you today?" with a polite "Fine, thank you." We arrange to meet in my office at 12:30 and she agrees to pass the word along to Daniel, the treasurer.

Earlier this morning, I sat for a few seconds staring at my computer, watching my own personal mission statement march across the screen, hoping I could live up to it today.

Caring Profoundly, Enacting Community, Inspiring Inquiry, Illuminating Possibility

Two summers ago, I composed these phrases for my screensaver during a workshop on "visioning." I don't recall what motivated me to give up the four June days for this topic, but I knew I needed to re-focus after the Columbine tragedy. The workshop refreshed me for the final two years, reminding me why I had walked through the door marked Principal in the first place.

Much of the time, the stream of events, kids, and conversations just flows forward, finding its own channel. Today, riding that flow, I'll make many more small choices than big decisions. Decisions are more administrative than choices, more about the public yes/no, now/later, this/that. They are the more obvious currency of school leadership.

Choices are the corrections, amendments, right or left turns, and adjustments in vocal tone that I make in each of the thousand moments that make up a day. They are the tiny adjustments that come from the place where my individual disposition meets my life experiences. Fundamental to my doing of this job, these choices, these units of inclination, are the subatomic particles of daily decision-making. I wish I could say that I only make good choices. Like decisions, choices not only express ideals, knowledge, wisdom, and good intentions, but also reflect misunderstandings, blind spots, and prejudices.

Today, will I stonewall? Will I lie to anyone? Will I weasel to avoid doing something that I really don't want to do? And today, will impatience trail off into anger, my own particular defense against the frustration that can come from never finishing anything, from encountering one more thing I'm supposed to pretend is other than what it is? Maybe.

My own history tells me that, without intending it, I might, on any day, display impatience or show less kindness or cordiality than a situation calls for. And I'll most likely listen less well than I should. Years ago, a teacher's comment on an anonymous survey told me that she noticed me drifting off in the middle of conversations, getting a far-away look in my eyes, picking at my cuticles, impatient to move on before I heard what she had to say. Since then, I have pushed myself not to withdraw and not to put myself out of range of someone else's needs. But it has not been easy, and I have not always succeeded.

For all my experience, I have come very slowly, and often in the wake of painful mistakes, to understand something fundamental about the work of a principal— that it's about relationships, about managing two hundred conversations of varying lengths across the course of a day. It's about maintaining composure, patience, and kindness while staying available not only to kids, teachers, parents, and your boss, but also to the central office workers who stop by without phoning ahead, to the pastor of the new church who wants to rent space in the building, and to the school psychologist who needs to add a puzzling child to your special needs class. *Understanding* this is not enough.

My Late 1960s

From the time I could walk and talk, my mother and father made sure I knew there was a university in town. At that university, I would study history and English and anthropology, aiming to graduate in the spring of 1968.

During my junior year, just before I turned 20, I took a semester off from college and moved to Massachusetts to see if the relationship with my boyfriend John was serious or not. Full of adolescent logic, I explained it this way to my mother: John *needed* me to type his MIT senior thesis. A year or two later, the onset of feminism might have cautioned me against this, but in 1967, traditional romantic expectations won out.

John found me a job at the MIT bookstore and a drab room in a three-decker on Kirkland Street. The house had a communal kitchen in the basement and, down the hall, a shared bathroom with a claw-foot tub. Weekends, John would pick me up and take me to the apartment he'd rented with friends in Stoneham, a town that I could not reach without a car.

A few weeks into my job at the MIT bookstore, I met a dark-haired girl clerking in General Books. Cheryl was filling time between being a VISTA Volunteer in New York City and going back to college. We started spending our lunch hours together. On some paydays, we crossed campus to a student café where we would split an order of fries to go with her hot dog and my cheeseburger. One day, after we'd found a table and put down our lunch trays, Cheryl dug into her Indian tapestry bag and pulled out a paperback book.

"You've *got* to read this."

I saw that underneath the word SUMMERHILL was printed the subtitle: *A Radical Approach to Child Rearing*. With no intention to raise children any time soon, and not sure that my progressive instincts were *radical*, I tried to hand the book back, but Cheryl insisted. I didn't want to insult the only friend I had found in Cambridge, so *Summerhill* went home with me in the bottom of my green book bag.

That night, I heated up some lentil soup in the downstairs kitchen and carried the bowl back upstairs. I pulled *Summerhill* out of the bag and, between spoonfuls of soup, skimmed the Table of Contents. I saw that Part III was about sex, an odd topic for school. I started there, with sex, and figured I could go back to the beginning later if I felt like it.

Over the next week, I moved from section to section, reading about children who could learn what and when they wanted to, children who helped make the rules of their "free" school. I'd never considered the possibility that young children could make some of the decisions in school. Reading *Summerhill* gave me a Eureka sort of a week, a short span of days in which my life peacefully but thoroughly rearranged itself. I would become a teacher, something I had resisted each of the thousand times my mother had suggested it.

In 1967, girls who went to college were not yet expected to have goals. I figured on marrying someone with a goal and an income that would support a family. I studied history and literature and anthropology because I *liked* them, and now I'd find a way to study education. Within the month, I decided that instead of using my major to teach high school history, I would teach little kids, maybe third graders. Elementary school, I concluded, was where everything began.

Today, 8:56 a.m.

Still hoping to be on time for my 9 o'clock observation, I walk back to the office with no more stops. From my cluttered desktop I grab a pen and a yellow writing pad and turn to leave, but my secretary, Susie, is blocking my way. Susie gestures with her eyes toward the front counter and says in her business voice that a man from School Security *wishes* to speak with me. Right now, I do not want to talk with someone who has just shown up and who *wishes* to see me. I really want to visit, need to visit, the restroom in the two minutes before the observation I've scheduled with Mrs. Currier.

I have scheduled this observation because the State of Arizona requires that I set aside an official half hour each semester to watch every teacher teach and to witness kids learning. A very punctual person, Mrs. Currier expects me in her room in two minutes to observe her lesson.

I have never seen this school security guy before. Late forties, five-feet-eight, one-eighty. His tan windbreaker squeezes his shoulders in a way that makes him look a little like a bulldog. He must be one of the retired cops the district hired after Columbine. Even if he's just driving around meeting principals today, he's picked a bad time. He lays a sheet of paper on the counter and smacks his palm down on it. "You sent this report."

When I give him a puzzled look, he slides the sheet of paper a couple inches toward my side of the counter. It's the alert I sent in three weeks ago on one of our fourth graders who's been swinging between moody isolation and defiant shout-outs. About a month ago, Bradley's teacher found him drawing guns, knives, and hypodermic needles. When she asked about the drawings, Bradley stuck the papers inside his desk and refused to talk.

Late last fall, Bradley got kicked out of the once-a-week gifted class after too many noisy outbursts. In the past two months, his teacher has called the office five times to get help calming him down. Even though Ms. Burnett is new to teaching and is slow to pick up my suggestions about organizing some of her lessons, she is kind to her students and doesn't complain about every little thing, so I jump when she asks for help.

Now, three weeks after I sent in Bradley's drawings, this officer drops by with no warning. If I take time to talk to him, I won't see Mrs. Currier start her lesson, something that matters to both of us. She is orderly and precise and will have planned a dynamic introduction to the lesson and she will begin promptly at 9:00. I don't ask the officer why the drawings are suddenly urgent today, after three weeks of sitting on someone's desk. That would only entangle me in an unwinnable debate.

"Sorry," I say, "I'm already late."

Frowning at a principal who will not sit down with him when he has shown up at her request, he thrusts his card at me. "Call me when you decide you have time." The fact that I'll be retiring in fifty-three days makes this hurt both more and less. Less, because I won't have to put up with much more of this kind of baloney, and more because this morning I'll arrive late for my very last observation of one of the best teachers I've ever known.

CHAPTER 5
I AM A TEACHER

1967–1970, Cambridge and Tucson

IN THE LATE SUMMER OF 1967, with things no more settled with John than when I'd arrived in the winter, I came home to Tucson to finish up my history degree. I still planned to be a teacher, but I'd have to graduate first and then find the time and place to take the education courses. I hadn't really figured this out by the time I finished up and left Tucson for Cambridge again in June.

I found summer work on a research project in Cambridge, and in September got a new job answering phones and typing letters for two professors in Harvard's Graduate School of Education. My desk was in a high-traffic lobby area, which let me meet the students and professors and listen in on hundreds of conversations. It was all new to me, and I soaked it up. But I wanted to teach, not roll sheets of paper in and out of a typewriter.

By December, I'd applied for Harvard's master's degree program in teaching. My acceptance letter arrived in April, around the same time students protesting the Vietnam War occupied University Hall. Campus life was almost immediately taken over by the Student Strike of 1969. At work each day, I traded the latest news and rumors with the graduate students, most of whom still showed up for classes even though Harvard College was in turmoil. I planned to leave the secretarial job at the end of June to begin my master's program apprentice-teaching in a summer school. Then I'd have two semesters of courses and another stretch of student-teaching.

During the twelve months I studied for my master's degree, Neil Armstrong walked on the moon and President Nixon announced the beginning of a five-year goodbye to Vietnam. When I was nearly finished, on May 4, 1970, national guardsmen in Ohio shot and killed four Kent State University students. The straitlaced, high-heeled teacher who ran the public school classroom where I was interning didn't say a word when I wore my red armband to school a couple of days that week.

My first teaching job came through a friend on the board of a district on the outskirts of Tucson. The week before school started, one of my new colleagues invited me to a planning meeting at her apartment. Arriving a few minutes early, I found my teammates already sitting around the dining room with glasses of iced tea. Once I had some tea and a seat at the table, they explained our program: At Walker Elementary, teachers taught in teams and children learned in mixed-age groups. Instead of rows of individual classrooms along corridors, Walker had huge learning pods with folding walls. The five of us would meet our 150 first and second graders in two of these work areas.

I would not teach the same group of kids all day. Each of us would start the morning with our home-room kids, a mixture of first and second graders, then trade the children around in both smaller and larger groups. These groups might have kids from just one grade, for reading, math, and writing, or from more than one grade, for social studies, science, and physical education. And sometimes we would all sit cross-legged on the carpeted floor.

Eager to be part of the team, I kept suggesting things I had heard or read about. Fresh from Cambridge, Massachusetts, and a practice-teaching stint in which I'd never really handled the whole class by myself, I said things like, "Maybe the kids don't have to line up for *everything*. Couldn't they just *walk* there?"

Marian, the senior member of the group, would say in a tone that was both pointed and diplomatic,

"Let's wait until we meet the kids to decide that," or "Wait until you've done this for a little while."

While Marian spoke up, the others just smiled. What I had gathered in theory, the Walker primary team had been practicing for several years. They had found that when you combine two grade levels, last year's first graders return as second graders experienced at the moves from room to room, from teacher to teacher. These older ones sweep the younger kids, the first graders, right into their routines.

During my three years at Walker, we were not willing to limit our first- and second-graders to the tradition of studying "home" and "the community" in social studies. Our kids learned how a region's geography and climate affected the people's choices of food, clothing, and shelter. We had our first, second, and, later, third graders studying primate behavior by role-playing baboons in a resting troop and in a defensive troop. Parents told us that their children hated to miss school and demanded to attend even when they were too ill to leave home.

In the same way our second graders initiated our first graders each year, my team initiated me, the newcomer, into a complex profession where most beginners flounder behind a closed door for a year or three before finding their balance. During my time on the Walker primary team, I *liked* my students, even loved and protected some of them who struggled with school or home issues, but I was young and single, hungry to know more about how children learned. I was also tired of lugging home an armload of math workbooks every day. I felt restless and began looking for a change. I told myself that three years was long enough to do anything. In June of 1973, I packed my Volkswagen bug for the return trip to Harvard, where I'd start work on my doctorate and where I never once thought of being a principal.

Today, 9:04 a.m.

After shaking off the security guy and visiting the restroom, I slip into Mrs. Currier's class almost five minutes late. I find her just finishing up her introduction of today's learning centers and of the visiting adults who'll help with these. Teams of four or five children seat themselves at work stations made from flat-top desks pushed together. Only Mrs. Currier seems to notice my arrival, and she nods in silent welcome. From a brief conversation yesterday, I know that today's lesson is part of a three-week study of how people live with various disabilities.

Wesley sits with three other children at a low table. Brown-haired and blue-eyed, he is taller than most of his classmates. The youngest in a large family, Wesley likes to annoy girls his age by tapping on their desks, marking their papers with a pencil, or commenting under his breath about their clothing. I don't like him and work hard to hide this from him and from his family.

Today, a volunteer mom is guiding Wesley's group. Big sheaves of paper that I take to be Braille books fill the flat workspace in front of them. Along with the others, Wesley seems to be listening, but I notice him sliding his finger back and forth between pages of one of the fat books. When I give him a look, Wesley meets my eyes and then looks away. He stops moving his finger but doesn't take it out of the book.

I circle the room for the next ten minutes or so, dipping into each group. A team working without adult help brainstorms questions to ask tomorrow's guest speaker, a female dentist who works from a wheelchair. I trust that the teacher has guided the children to compose questions about the dentist's life on the job instead of asking the old standbys about her favorite color and food. A second parent helper, a dad, teaches a lesson about sign language and I watch the children try to imitate his signals.

Suddenly the door flies open and a boy from the class next door announces "I gotta be in here on time-out until 9:30." He smirks as he looks around to see what's going on and notices the sign-language group seated at his usual time-out spot. Mrs. Currier's kids know to say nothing, to avoid eye contact. Aware that I'm not just sitting in my office waiting for kids to be sent, teachers make these arrangements with neighboring classes to time-out some of their troublemakers for up to a half hour. In her soft voice, Mrs. Currier says, "Just take your regular chair. You'll be with the sign language group."

The newcomer manages to knock the chair over and then clown-fumbles to set it upright. At last he twists down and sideways into the seat, managing to screech one of the metal chair feet against the tile floor. Mrs. Currier turns away from him and pulls her group more tightly around her. The dad running the sign-language group joins in the general ignoring and continues with the lesson.

A few minutes later, while the groups move to their next locations, I catch the time-out boy trying to pull Wesley into some kind of discussion. Wesley rebuffs him in a loud voice, managing to draw the attention of the adults in the room while more or less doing the right thing. The outburst dies before any of us gets sucked in.

Mrs. Currier's talent at civilizing and then teaching kids seems to me other-worldly, a gift I seriously doubt can be packaged and taught to her peers. Because of the personal relationship she creates with each child and the caring community she establishes each year within her classroom, I have assigned to her class one or two more volatile children than is strictly fair. This year's group is one of her most turbulent ever. By this seventh month of the school year, an outsider would probably think she has the best kids in the school.

I join the group that's settled on the rug that defines the reading area. Against the hum of the other work centers, the five children lean in so their heads almost touch. Each of them holds a photocopied article on the history of Braille. A traditionalist might not recognize this as a reading group. The material is too authentic, the level challenging. In the brittle and arbitrary way these things are figured for tests, scores show that Mrs. Currier's kids make a fifteen-month gain in the school year they are with her. And her kids end up loving to read and write.

Mrs. Currier introduces the "story," as the kids insist on calling it, by first pointing to the title and then to the picture on the first page. "Lots of hard words," a blond-haired boy mutters at the same time the teacher asks her group, "What do you think this article is going to be about?"

Raising hands and taking turns, children say, "blind people," "those dot letters," and "reading when you can't see."

Over the months of this school year, Mrs. Currier has polished their reading-group performance, and they hardly ever try to drown each other out with shouted answers. Here, by design, the quick-and-impulsive claim no advantage over the reflective or the shy.

She turns to a child who has not said anything yet. "Graciela, what do you think?" The teacher goes on to spin each child's response positively, using it to build momentum in the direction she has set. Even Wesley rises to the occasion, holding it together beyond what I thought possible. As they near the end of the article, Mrs. Currier says, "Let's read page five together."

I wish I could say that my visit today is a true instance of the principal's basic duty, instructional leadership. But this teacher is way ahead of me. Every school will have one or a dozen teachers more experienced, and just plain better in the classroom, than the principal is or ever was. Yes, I taught school once, but I got restless after three years, not long enough to master the job.

After about thirty-five minutes of observing her groups as they rotate through the study centers and the reading lesson with their teacher, I slip out the door. On my way out, I see Mrs. Currier look up at me and at the clock to make sure I've stayed for the required half hour.

Tucson, August 1977
In the cavernous room that served as both auditorium and cafeteria of one of Tucson's oldest school buildings, I filled a Styrofoam cup from the coffee urn and backed up against the wall next to the refreshment table. I watched a tall blonde woman dump a plastic spoonful of whitener into her own cup and stir it in. I could not remember her name or her title from the round of introductions at the beginning of the meeting, just that she supervised some part of the curriculum. She was probably twenty years older than I was then, which would have made her about fifty.

All at once, she shouldered up to me and leaned over sideways so that her mouth came just a little too close to my ear. "*Our* university offers a perfectly *fine* education. Many *fine* teachers graduate from *this* university." *Thisssss universsssity.*

An hour earlier, I'd been introduced to the gathering of teacher-specialists as a doctoral student who'd be their newest program evaluator. I'd be the third member of a team who would be scrutinizing their work in federally funded school programs. I was younger than all but a couple of these teachers. They had taught kids in classrooms for years and had worked their way up through the system while I'd gone to graduate school in a faraway state. I was too new and too young to worry about the fact that I would be watching them work, measuring their work, judging their work, writing about their work, yet not working as one of them. I told my supervisors that I'd spend a year, finish my dissertation and leave for a job as a professor somewhere.

I worked days at the school district's headquarters and nights at home writing my doctoral thesis. My new colleague Helen was teaching me how to evaluate the federal Title I programs, and, perhaps more importantly, how not to condescend to the teachers. I shared a tiny office at district headquarters with a third evaluator, a kind man who helped me apply my graduate school statistics classes to the job in front of me.

Helen took me to schoolhouses in Tucson's central city to meet principals and teachers. The buildings were older than the red-brick schools of my own childhood, with white or tan stucco exteriors and central patios ringed by classrooms. Some still had original woodwork and colorful tile trim that showed off their Mexican heritage. As winter came, and I worked long evenings on my thesis, I didn't have time to scout around for a university job.

I had chosen a thesis topic on the earliest stages of reading, a topic that, contrary to custom, was not part of a professor's grant-funded research. That would have been the more usual, and perhaps wiser, approach. In March, at a moment when I was not sure I'd finish in time for June graduation, I learned that the Tucson schools had money to pay me for a second year if I wanted to stay. I asked for a day or two to think it over, and after a tearful and pessimistic phone call with one of my thesis committee members, I agreed to another year in the evaluator job.

CHAPTER 6
THE PRINCIPAL SAYS

1978, Tucson

AFTER I'D HANDED IN my thesis and bought a plane ticket for my June graduation, I needed to compare some of our Title I second graders with some second graders who *didn't* get the extra help with reading. Cragin Elementary, the school where I'd skipped down the block to start first grade back in 1953, was just above the low-income cutoff for Title I, so it could serve as a comparison to the program schools. I called to make an appointment with the principal, Mr. Rhoads.

I thought asking for the test scores was routine, that this visit was merely a formality. After all, the teachers and principals in the Title I schools always did the extra work needed to keep their federal money and they didn't complain to me, their evaluator, about it. I thought I'd stated my request clearly enough to Cragin's principal, but the closest Mr. Rhoads came to "yes" was a cautious and slightly hostile "maybe."

After work that day, I went looking for my friend Dave, an assistant superintendent whose office was around two corners and up a hallway from mine. Dave was a dozen years older and a few layers above me in district pecking order, but we had gotten to know each other through a close mutual friend. His office window framed the mountain range that rises abruptly from Tucson's north side, while my office window overlooked an air shaft. Taller than me by a few inches, Dave looked squared off without being stocky. His dark brown hair showed its first specks of gray. I knew that his gruff "just do it" covered a generous heart and a questing mind.

When I poked my head in to see if he was there, Dave looked up and said, "What's up, kid?"

"Bill Rhoads is what's up. All I wanted was test scores from his second grades. He said he had to ask the *teachers* first."

Dave said, "Caroliner, you researchers are full of shit!"

Dave had called me "Caroliner" since the day we'd met years earlier. Now, he got up from his chair and sat back against the front edge of his desk with his arms crossed. At first I thought his "full of shit" comment was more of the joking around he always did with me, that he was giving me a light elbow in the ribs before showing the sympathy I deserved. Then he volunteered another opinion.

"Bill Rhoads is a great principal. He's just doing his job. He's *supposed* to protect his teachers. Kid, like I said about researchers . . ."

Dave stopped, made sure I was looking at his face, then went on, "The good principals do their best to protect their teachers from all the central office crap we drop on their heads. And the principal says what gets done in the school."

But I had never wanted to be a principal, had not even thought about it. I had already detoured into a school district from what should have been a university career. Now someone who was smart and experienced, *and* who cared about me, was telling me bluntly that I was not going to save the world through clever and conclusive research.

I soon found that only a few of my doctoral courses would help me get certified as a school administrator. To be a principal, I'd need five or six more classes along with many hours of internship. Three months after I'd picked up my doctoral diploma, I registered for General School Administration at the University of Arizona. A decent raise kept me in my evaluator job for a third year, and in 1980 a big federal grant allowed me to stay in the district, doing research in bilingual language assessment.

Aiming first at a certificate that would let me supervise a staff, but not run a school, I registered for night classes at the university each semester. I did not have a master plan, just a more pronounced drift. In my classes, I learned a little budget management and a little school law. When I had that first-level certificate, I got a job supervising professional support staff, a centralized office of psychologists, social workers, occupational therapists, and a few other people whose work involved traveling from school to school.

During my second year at this job, I enrolled in the class called The Principalship. This course aimed at the ideal situation in which a principal has plenty of time to operate as the instructional leader, the phrase that still names the official priority of our work. Meanwhile, my busy days supervising people who worked with special needs children kept me a step removed from my own commitments to teachers and classrooms. The idea of myself as a principal remained abstract, and I still would have said I was increasing my options, just in case.

Today, 9:39 a.m.

When I leave Mrs. Currier's lesson, I step into the room next door so I can check off another visit for today. This morning's birthday girl conducts a class meeting that seems to be about some kids tripping others during recess. Kids who were tripped tell how it felt to fall down and how it felt to be tricked by someone they trusted. Next, some kids promote over-the-top punishments for the trippers, like no PE for the rest of the year, but the teacher coaches them to a milder solution. If they can resolve their PE flap at this level, it's one more life skill for them and one less referral to me.

Next, I need to find two kids from the witness list I made when Mitchell and I talked about his mother's phone call. As I walk into the room, a murmur rises from the class. I smile and say, "Hi. I need to borrow Greg for a few minutes." I've forgotten that there's a substitute teacher in this class today. This sub, one of our best, covers absences at Brichta at least once a week and actually tries to teach the kids something. She tells me she doesn't like working in this class because, even three-quarters of the way through the year, the kids seem uncertain about classroom routines and argue constantly about what they should be doing. I had to beg her to take this group today.

The sub looks around and says, "I think Greg just went to the cafeteria for orchestra with the other kids." I notice the six empty desks and realize that orchestra does not begin for fifteen more minutes. The orchestra teacher always runs in on the dot of 10:00 from one of his other schools, and it's only 9:45. I wonder how early the kids left. I start to picture a small herd of children, violin cases in hand, roaming the halls or banging on the keys of the old upright piano in the cafeteria.

Wincing inside at one more round of schoolchild vs. substitute teacher, I stop myself from explaining it to the sub, and head out to find the escapees. From just outside the cafeteria doors, I hear competing versions—one high, one low—of "Mary Had a Little Lamb" being hammered out on the out-of-tune piano. They have forgotten to post a lookout, so I'm on top of them before they see me coming.

I almost laugh at their suddenly-contrived meekness, at the dozen round eyes focused oh-so-innocently on me. One girl leads off. "Greg said Mr. Robertson told us to come early to practice today." I peel Greg and Cheralyn, my two witnesses, away from the group and shoo the others back toward the classroom. They have missed ten minutes of math, and their re-entry will scramble what's left of the substitute's lesson.

1986, Miller School

Nine years and three jobs after I had first evaluated federal programs, my central office job was being reorganized away. By then, I'd earned my principal's certificate and my supervisor asked if I'd consider taking on a school. Still without a master plan, I regarded this offer as a door I might as well enter as long as it was being held open. I imagined spending three years as a principal. That should, I thought, be enough time to figure it out, even master it, leave my mark, and move on to the next thing, probably central office again, perhaps supervising principals.

Filling out my transfer form, I thought back to the schools I'd visited over the last several years. I made a list of the ones that had seemed businesslike and positive, with teachers who seemed to enjoy their work, who treated children well, and whose rooms were filled with inquiry and discovery. At a practical level, I preferred not to have to face a school in turmoil or with a miserable staff right away, and I had seen some of these on my visits. As a beginner, I figured I could learn by working in a school that was running well, and I was thrilled when the School Board appointed me to Miller.

When I called my dad to tell him about my new job, he said, "Good for you, honey! That shouldn't be too hard. All you have to do is ring the bells."

On the Friday before the Monday that I started my life as a principal, I picked up my school keys at an out-of-the-way industrial building that held a collection of school district offices. Back in the car, I drove for twenty minutes southwest out of town, passing the last Safeway, the last Chinese restaurant, and the last McDonald's. When I slowed for the turn into Miller's parking lot, I passed on my left the backyards of modest yellow and tan masonry houses. To my right stood a closely packed row of stuccoed townhomes.

Recently added to Tucson's collection of red-brick schoolhouses, Miller's dark red block walls and updated design had already won an architectural award. The building sat on several acres that had been leveled with trucked-in dirt. Later, we would find this dirt suitable for archeological practice-digging even though all the pot shards had been completely dislocated from where they'd originally fallen. On that first morning, I would look out a back door across a couple of miles of desert and see Tucson's white-domed trademark, the San Xavier del Bac mission church.

Miller's single floor of classrooms, offices, library, and cafeteria clustered around a central patio. Two raised planters held half-grown trees, and pyracantha bushes sprouted here and there from openings in the courtyard's concrete floor. With my new keys, I entered the door marked OFFICE, and then unlocked the inner room, the one marked PRINCIPAL. I cranked open the blinds, or at least the three sets that worked, and looked out to the empty central patio. Soon enough, this space would overflow with six hundred children, twenty-seven teachers, two secretaries, four cafeteria ladies, a part-time nurse, two fulltime custodians and a third one who worked four hours a day, various hourly monitors and teaching assistants, plus visiting parents.

I sat down on the armless swivel chair that didn't match the brown wooden principal's desk. I slid open the desk's drawers one at a time. Laid out neatly in the upper right-hand drawer were new pens and pencils, paper clips, a stapler, and scissors. Alongside those tools was a fresh pad of lined paper and a red leatherette date book that showed one week of the school year on each set of facing pages. The second drawer was empty, but dusted and cleaned, waiting.

The bottom drawer, the big one, held a dozen brightly colored file folders. Their typed labels announced *Teachers, PTO, Test Scores, Staff, Building and Grounds,* and assorted other topics. The folder labeled *Handbook* might as well have said *Pandora's Box.* In this folder I found a slim booklet made from legal-size sheets of paper printed on both sides, folded in half, and then stapled inside a heavy blue paper cover. *Miller School Handbook, 1986–87.* This booklet revealed to the families and kids—and to me—how Miller School did business. I felt a surge of relief to find that the previous principal had put together this year's handbook, something I didn't even realize you were supposed to have.

I soaked up the first half of the *Handbook* in the same eager way I had once read to my mother the list of school supplies I needed for third grade. The booklet listed the PTO officers, showed the names and room numbers of the teachers, and suggested safe footwear options for the students. The *Handbook* laid out school hours, lunch prices and times, and explained what to do if your child needed to take medicine at school. It went on to warn that children wouldn't be allowed to use the office phone to make social plans and that the office wouldn't issue loans to replace lost or forgotten lunch money. Instead, a peanut butter sandwich and a portion of milk would be provided so no child would go hungry.

The second half of the *Handbook* sat me right up in my chair. Until now, I had managed to avoid the fact that I would be Miller School's Disciplinarian-in-Chief. These pages spelled out the school rules and detailed what would happen the first time a child broke the rule, the next time, and the third, which in some ideal universe was supposed to be the last time. Reading through the *Handbook's* "policies," as the behavior rules were called, my beginner's mind grasped one concept here, the rules. I just needed to learn the rules.

Today, 9:49 a.m.

In the corridor with Cheralyn and Greg, I ask Cheralyn to move away a little so I can speak semi-privately with Greg. I suspect that, like Ricky, Greg will claim that he is trying to stop a fight and that peace is all he ever had in mind. I'll get more out of him if I appeal to his self-importance.

"What's going on with Caleb and Mitchell?" I ask, pitching my voice to suggest that I have absolutely no idea, and that I am relying on him to fill me in.

"I heard Caleb say he was so mad at Mitchell that he wanted to kick his butt," Greg answers, and then quickly adds, "but I told Caleb he wasn't supposed to fight." After a few more questions and answers that lead me nowhere, I send him back to class and walk over to Cheralyn.

I fish. "What do you know about some business with Mitchell and Caleb?"

Jutting her jaw and lifting her chest, Cheralyn says, "They said they were going to kick Mitchell's butt for no reason!"

"Who said?" I asked.

"Those guys. You know. Caleb's friends."

"Which ones?" I need to hear her say the names.

"Greg told me that Caleb said he was gonna kick Mitchell's butt."

"I need to know what you heard Caleb say."

"Nothing, but Greg said . . ."

Growing impatient, I swallow a couple of times to get the clench out of my jaw. I might need Cheralyn as a friendly witness some other time, so I smile when I thank her and send her back to class for the five minutes that remain until orchestra begins.

I arrive at the office just in time to watch second-grader Patrick slide off one of the green reception chairs in front of the counter and pretend to be dead on the floor. Susie, my secretary and right arm, says, "There's a note in your basket," and I hope she means a note about Patrick and not a second thing I've got to squeeze into this shard of time.

> Patrick has been singing loudly and won't stop. The other children are having trouble getting their work done.

Patrick has annoyed pretty much everyone this year, but his teacher usually handles this level of disruption. Either she's in a bad mood today or there's more to this than the note suggests. I really don't have time to figure out which.

Patrick exhales loudly and says, "I'm bored."

"Then you're probably ready to go back to class without singing. Am I right?"

"Yes. You are *right!*" he says, as if I've answered the million-dollar question.

I send him back without testing the strength of his reply.

On the second note in my wire basket, I recognize Mrs. Sorensen's distinctive script and her preference for complete sentences even in informal situations.

> Jenifer is very sad this morning because she just found out she doesn't get to visit with her mother and brothers this afternoon.

I pocket this one for later and leave for Mr. McElroy's portable.

CHAPTER 7
SURROUNDED

1986, Miller School

WHEN SCHOOL STARTED IN September, I found myself surrounded by *hundreds* of people who did not call ahead or show up one at a time. The kids streamed in on buses, on foot, or by car in the half hour before the electronic class bell sounded at 8:00. Before, during, and after school, these kids, some of their parents, and a staff of over fifty adults clamored for scheduled and unscheduled attention. Any time I was not in the classrooms, playground, or hallways, I was supposed to be in my office with the door open, busy enough to earn my salary and un-busy enough to greet anyone who stopped by.

In those early weeks on the job, I struggled with my shyness, with my preference for structure, and with something even worse. *I hated it* when people dropped in expecting to see me. I dreaded kids showing up at any moment, sent by teachers fed up with them. When parents stopped by with a question or a complaint, I pushed my secretary to set an appointment a day or so later. As a teacher, professor, or researcher, I might have avoided exposure to this noisy everything-at-once. I felt desperately alone, *one* of me and *all* of *them*.

When you are appointed principal, it's a little like when you get married. On both occasions, people who've already done it fuss over you as if you've accomplished something really big. Can anyone tell a bride that the marriage will be a lot harder than the wedding? Like married people, principals with some experience won't tell you how many times in the first year they tripped or cried or wondered if they'd ever figure it out.

Before I landed at Miller, I had not considered how I, Caroline, would show up in my new role. I had a blurry picture that combined my own childhood principals, the one I had worked for as a teacher, and the many I'd met while working for the school district, but I could not visualize myself in this group photo. I hoped that Caroline Tompkins, the *person*, would get by with her own streaked blonde, all-cotton, flat-heeled look. I knew also that in the mid-1980s it was safe to bring along with me to the job my knowledge—and my opinions—about teaching and learning. I would play the part of head teacher, sharing my ideas, listening to everyone's suggestions and making decisions jointly with the whole faculty. What I failed to bring into the picture was the whirlwind that school can be even when everything is operating normally.

Life in my central office jobs, both research and supervisory, had been measured by the half hour. Now, I sometimes felt lucky to have two minutes to start on one thing, to deal with one person's needs, to communicate one thought, before two or three more of these demanded my attention. I thought I would never get used to it. Each night, I fell asleep early, before 10 o'clock, then woke between 3 and 4 a.m. On some of those mornings, I managed to fall back asleep until the alarm rang at 6:00.

One October day, a playground monitor's note said, "Leo shoved Arnie and then kicked dirt onto his shoes. He called Arnie's mother a bad name." The *Handbook* told me that this event, Leo's third referral, earned one of his parents a face-to-face meeting with the principal. My phone call to set up the meeting with his mother seemed routine. Any concern in her tone didn't register as antagonism toward me.

But the next morning she stood sobbing in my office.

"You don't have any children of your own, so how could you know how I feel? You don't know what it's like to hear this stuff about your kid. The whole neighborhood knows you don't have any kids and you don't care about ours." Rivulets of eye makeup ran down her cheeks while she let me have it.

Within five minutes of stepping into my office, Leo's mother dried her tears, tissued off the streaks of mascara, and walked out. We didn't manage to discuss Leo's behavior, but by the time she left, that seemed beside the point. Shaken by her outburst and not completely sure what had happened, I sat down at my desk. At first I latched on to the part about the "whole neighborhood." I was too new in my job to know that "the whole neighborhood" as often as not meant someone's next door neighbor and the sister-in-law who sent her kids to Catholic school, where plenty of the teachers didn't have kids either.

When I started as Miller's principal, I had not taught children in classrooms for thirteen years. In the schools I visited for evaluation, the children were someone else's responsibility. In my personal life, children didn't exist beyond the four preschoolers who belonged, two each, to my sister and to my friend Linda. Whenever I got tired of one of these kids, all I had to do was go home. Another friend relayed what her eight-year-old son said when she'd told him about my new job at Miller. *"How can Caroline be a principal? She doesn't even like kids."*

On the rare occasions when I saw the boy who said that, I found him bouncy and annoying, something I tolerated for the sake of my friendship with his mother. In his assessment of my prospects as principal, he was on to something: No one who knew me was likely to say, "Caroline just loves kids!" I didn't like messiness, neediness, or clamor. Children—*learners*—in the abstract were one thing, but up close with runny noses and all that yelling and running around, they were quite another. I liked to schedule things, to set appointments, and to have a predictable working life. I still do.

In those first two months, I sat down at my office table with moms or dads of at least a dozen kids to talk about playground fights or classroom eruptions. With the *Handbook* spread open in front of us, I pointed to the relevant rule and recited the details of the complaint I'd received from a teacher or monitor. Even if some parents quibbled a bit over the particulars, they almost always said they would work with the child to do better, and off they'd go.

So far, my connection with parents had been more careful than cordial. On the good side, one or another of Miller's PTO officers showed up each day. They were friendly and supportive and never asked for favors. Later I suspected that my predecessor had rigged last spring's parent-organization election so that I'd have at least a few angels my first year. The friendly visits of these PTO officers gave me flashes of hope that I could manage the matter of *parents*, yet I stayed uneasy. I could not put myself in the place of the moms and dads who loved their unruly and sometimes violent children, children who seemed to me not only annoying, but who also might hurt someone with little warning.

Even after my long-ago three years of teaching, I did not understand how much emotion drives the complex engagement between parents and children. And, whether you look at the relationship between educators and parents as chess, dodge ball, or a family fight, misinformation and misunderstanding abound. My administration courses had not bothered with Rule One of talking to children's parents, the rule that says *Caring is essential to your job, so make certain they know that you, too, care about their children.*

I grasped little of how my middle-classness, my obstinate reasonableness about behavior rules, and my personal discomfort with the clamor of children would keep kids' parents at a distance from me. An independent single woman, I was the center of my own gravity, clueless about that dramatic shift of emotional weight that comes when a first baby arrives. All more of what I didn't know I didn't know.

Today, 10:04 a.m.

"SIT DOWN!" Norma bellows at the kids around her. I have joined in progress Mr. McElroy's map lesson.

Big for her age, with naturally curly auburn hair billowing around her face, Norma wears an oversized pink T-shirt with a cat face embossed on the front. Despite the efforts of her teacher, Norma has yet to find a tone between holler and whine. When the other kids in her group don't follow orders, Norma downshifts to a whine. "Mr. Mac, they won't sit with me!"

I never know what the teachers tell the kids before I come in to observe. Every once in a while, teachers have marked my arrival by telling the kids, "Show Dr. Tompkins what we were doing this morning to get ready for this." And then I watch some gimmicky lesson with no connection to what they were learning yesterday or what they'll be doing tomorrow.

At both Miller and Brichta, teachers assumed at first that I wanted to see them stand up in front of the room imparting knowledge to well-behaved children. I believe that within a year or two in each place, I managed to convince all of them that I wanted to see *learning*, the real business of school, no matter how they inspired or provoked it. Teachers like Mr. McElroy and Mrs. Currier, and others at Brichta and at Miller, showed me how I'd want to do it if I found myself back at the beginning.

Like Mrs. Currier's students an hour ago, Mr. McElroy's have sorted themselves out into fours and fives around clusters of desks. Now, Mr. McElroy moves to a spot near Norma and speaks to her, his voice softened in order to pull some of the energy out of her indignation. "Well, maybe standing up is a better way for everyone to see the map."

Before Norma can argue with him, Mr. McElroy moves away to help a boy and girl from the special needs class get included—if not welcomed—in groups. Each day, these two children from Ms. Langer's Cross-Categorical class come in for social studies, a practice that falls under the technical term "inclusion," and that used to be called "mainstreaming."

If these "included" kids sat with the same groups every day, life could stay consistent and familiar for them. But their almost nonexistent reading stirs resentment in any team that hosts one or the other for more than a few weeks. It looks like Mr. McElroy is putting them into new groups today. He and I have talked about how not-easy is this decision, and I don't judge him.

Each team has unfolded an Arizona road map with a small chart in one corner showing distances and estimated times for driving between various pairs of cities. The groups also have a pre-printed list of items to find or calculate using the map, with blank spaces for writing the answers. The first team to hand Mr. McElroy a correct and legible finished product will win an extra fifteen minutes in the workshop corner dismantling the dead VCR.

As the groups more or less settle in, Steven still spacewalks around the room. A tawny child of mixed heritage, Steven's narrow face reveals neither emotion nor devilish intention. He doesn't look up at me as he explains himself in a robot-imitation tone. "I'm *look*-ing for my *back*-pack."

When the backpack turns up under his desk two seconds later, Steven acts surprised. His group, probably relieved at his late arrival, is moving forward with the map lesson, and they have answered the first three questions. The girl who is running things gives Steven a look as she moves aside to let him get a peek first at the questions and then at the map. She says, "We're on number four."

I see Steven pencil an oversized 7 on a scrap of paper. My copy of the questions tells me that seven asks for the driving time in hours and minutes between Phoenix and Yuma by way of Gila Bend. I watch Steven scratch out a calculation. From halfway across the room, I can see the big dark numerals **2** and **67** on the scrap of paper he pitches into the center of the map. He accompanies his gesture with crash-landing noises. No one picks up the slip of paper, and Steven grabs it back.

The teacher calls Steven to him and they talk briefly outside of my hearing. Pushing himself to please his teacher, Steven rejoins his group without immediately touching anything. While the girl leading the group writes the answers for item four, Steven bumps his body against one of the desks and says, "I've got seven here. Put my answer."

The girl leading the group gives him another look and says, "Just wait."

When I think Steven is containing himself and paying attention to his group's work on item five, his own drummer tells him to begin working on number eight.

Steven realizes that number eight requires some information from the reverse side of the map. He starts to turn the map over, but it tears as the pressure of another boy's elbow holds it against the table. The other kids manage to ignore this. It seems they'd rather lose the competition than give in to Steven's undermining. I say to them, "You guys are doing a great job figuring this out together."

The group leader smiles a little at my commonplace teacherish remark. These kids have practiced for months how to defend against Steven's disruption.

1986, Miller School

In mid-autumn of my first year, the district announced plans to open two new schools in neighborhoods not far from Miller. One-third of our six hundred kids would move to the new schools, and a corresponding one-third of our teachers would be cut loose to find other jobs within the district. This downsizing of Miller would throw the teachers and me into a subtle ballet of courtship and separation.

The teacher contract prescribed a complicated but orderly process to determine who would leave and who would stay. Even though anyone who left was guaranteed a job in another school, a move like this might still be unwelcome or unsettling. If exactly seven volunteered to leave, no one would have to be pushed out. If fewer than seven wanted to transfer, I would have to send away the newest—the least senior—teachers.

But what if *more* than seven wanted to go? What would that mean about *me*, still running far behind my predecessor, Mrs. Rice? Stories circulated about schools where half the faculty, or more, transferred out when they couldn't stand the principal. What could I do to make sure that by March most of them would want to stay?

I knew that I'd followed a master principal into this job. Kids, teachers, parents, *and* her superiors had all respected Mrs. Rice. Some teachers still mourned her departure, or at least that's how I took the insertion of "Elaine always . . . ." when they asked my opinion or permission. Any attempt at imitating her would have been comical, if not tragic, and wouldn't have captured the essence of her particular talent.

Mrs. Rice was at the same time both warmer and more composed than I in her manner, and she displayed her preference for order in details that I might not even notice, like making sure that finger marks were cleaned from the windows each day. Over time, I realized that Mrs. Rice's genius lay not just in her attention to detail, but also in the moment-to-moment tone of her conversations, in which she focused on the person in front of her and not on what she had to do next.

This was not something I could grasp from the *Miller School Handbook*. We all had to make the best of Mrs. Rice's departure.

Even though I knew I was supposed to be visiting classrooms regularly, I seemed always to have something urgent to do in the office. When I did stop by a classroom, I never stayed more than a minute or two. I told myself that I didn't want to bother the teachers. Whatever excuse I made, I felt shy and I feared doing the wrong thing even though I couldn't name what that might be. Later, a teacher who became my friend told me that in my first year at Miller, I walked around with such a serious expression on my face that people thought I was mad at them.

By late October, in spite of my shyness, I began to visit classrooms unannounced. For one thing, I discovered that I had fallen far behind in scheduling the required teacher observations. By then, I had also started buying lunch in the student cafeteria and carrying my tray to the staff lounge, where, over fish sticks or beefy mac, I sat and listened to the teachers' mid-day conversations. Sitting around one very large table, they would talk about the kids in their classes or about their own kids or their weekend plans. Maybe they thought I was spying or trying to disrupt their midday break. I'll never know what topics they avoided *because* I was there.

These meetings over lunch may have helped along a necessary familiarity between the teachers and me, but as a newcomer to principaling, I failed to reckon with some of the ways in which I could not just be one of the gang. From the beginning, people seemed to listen to me. They treated me well and said "yes" rather than "no." I was too new to realize that it was my title, *Principal,* more than the merit of what I said or did, that got parents to call me back, that made kids look up and settle down when I caught them acting rowdy, that pushed teachers to participate in staff meetings.

In the years since I'd left classroom teaching, I hadn't held a job that had the power to intimidate various categories of people the way this one did. I only felt a *little* authoritative, a *little* like the boss, and I didn't get that people said one thing to my face while they thought or did something else entirely. Naïve in the way the daughter of a powerful politician might be in thinking she is the object of respect in her own right, I didn't catch on that I hadn't earned the "yes" or the smile.

While I imagined I was being an earnest and determined version of myself, kids, teachers, staff, and parents looked at me as The Principal. Nevertheless, mistaking Miller Elementary School's habits of courtesy for some kind of leadership skill on my part kept me going in those early days. With the new schools and the staff reduction coming up, I realized that pushing big changes this first year was not going to inspire the

Miller teachers. I wasn't sure yet if Dave was right about the principal saying what happened in a school. So far, I had hired a couple of monitors and asked the librarian to tone down his overzealous scoldings of children who had overdue books. But the deeper meaning in Dave's words, *saying what happened*, would have to wait.

In the fall of that first year, I admired how Bonnie Hadley taught her third graders, but I didn't think she liked me very much. She would come to me asking permission to do things that were already within her authority, like arranging a special library project for her students. At the same time, she seemed to find frequent opportunities to say things like, "Hmmm. I wasn't sure. Mrs. Rice usually did it this way."

Still, I hoped she'd choose to stay at Miller when we had to cut staff in the spring. One day I decided to risk asking her advice about a field trip. She said it would be OK if I stopped in to see her after school. When I arrived at her room, she was busy with a pile of papers on her desk.

"Um, hi," she said, without a smile.

"Hi, Bonnie," I said, "Is it still OK for us to talk for a minute?"

She still didn't smile, but set her pencil down on the pile of papers in front of her. "Yes, sure." Lacking an invitation to sit down, I stood in front of her desk and started, "I heard that some years, all the third grades go together to a concert at the University, and I was wondering . . ."

Trying to hurry and not take more of her time than necessary, I couldn't quite make myself understood, or she was determined to misunderstand. Maybe Bonnie's blank expression reflected her already-made but not-yet-revealed decision to leave at the end of the year. Suddenly, without knowing why, I started to cry. While Bonnie maintained a posture of slight confusion, I hurried back to my office.

CHAPTER 8
LEARNING THE RULES

Today, 10:15 a.m.

TODAY I'M RELISHING Mr. McElroy's lesson, just as I did Mrs. Currier's. I'm pretty sure that Mr. McElroy runs his classroom the same way whether I'm watching or not. Even so, I think most kids behave at least a little differently when I'm in the room. Some hold themselves in, while others make sure to put on a show. I admire Mr. McElroy for succeeding with Steven and with Norma, for cheerfully including Ms. Langer's two kids for an hour each day.

Ten minutes into the map work, the groups have finished about half of the questions. I notice that her team has given the girl from Ms. Langer's class the job of looking for the wiggly blue lines that mark rivers, and she holds her face close to the map, following her moving finger with her eyes. Meanwhile, the boy from Ms. Langer's room sits unfocused, listless, edged aside by his group. I feel relieved that the girl seems involved, but I feel better when Mr. McElroy stops by and gently reconnects the boy with his group. In another part of the room, Norma and her teammates nearly bump heads as they bend over their map.

I'm still slipping in and out of the groups when, about twenty minutes into the lesson, one team races all together toward Mr. McElroy, shouting, "We won!"

Two of the runners actually bump into their teacher before thrusting the list into his hand. Mr. McElroy scans their sheet and tells them, "Go back and take another look at number seven."

Like Steven, this team hasn't converted the two hours and sixty-seven minutes into proper format. While they wrangle over what the problem might be, I'm distracted by red-faced Norma pursuing a teammate across the room, screeching, "Give it back!"

A boy on Norma's team has somehow managed to get the group's answer sheet out of her clutches to claim the win for their team. I just now catch on that a clever and quiet girl in Norma's group has led them to victory. She knows that Norma likes to hold the pencil more than she likes to figure out the answers, so the girl just tells Norma what to write.

In another couple of minutes, all the groups have handed in their sheets and Mr. McElroy declares a winner.

They holler and carry on as he announces the second and third place finishers as well. Because of disputes over completeness, actual time of submission, and so on, the kids disagree about how this should play out. For once Norma stays quiet, her group's victory leaving her nothing further to protest.

Mr. McElroy wants to make sure everyone understands why the right answers are the right answers. "OK, guys, settle down. Now listen to how we're going to do this. Each group is going to send someone up to explain how you got your answers. Shelley, come on up and show us number one." I remain a bit longer to hear the follow-up discussion and to make sure I've been there for the required thirty minutes.

I depart as they start on number six, so I miss hearing them analyze the sixty-seven-minute problem. That would have been fun, because Mr. McElroy wouldn't have told them the answer, but would have coached them through the solution. Another teacher who is miles ahead of me.

The note still lies in my pocket, the one about Jenifer and her sad day. I still need to see Caleb and Ricky before they go to lunch in an hour. Since the kindergartners head to the cafeteria at 10:40, I'll check on Jenifer first and then double back to catch my fourth graders.

1986–87, Miller School
Scrambling to learn where to stand and what to say during those first months at Miller, I was also

discovering the high-stakes game that teachers and principals play over children's behavior in the classroom. I had started out trying to manage situations the monitors brought me from the cafeteria and the playground. I didn't like stepping into the chaos of the cafeteria at lunchtime or dealing with boys who'd turned a mid-day soccer game into a fight. My stomach tightened each time a child brought matches to school, cursed a classmate, or mimicked the teacher during a boring lesson.

The *Miller School Handbook* referred to behavior in general terms, and the rules began to seem less focused than they had at the beginning, leaving me to scramble for answers while I was encountering entirely new questions. I was not just the enforcer-in-chief, but also had to *help* the teachers with kids who distracted and disrupted, or who lashed out with violence in the classroom. Too often I judged and evaluated before I cared or sympathized, taking rowdy children and their defensive parents as a personal insult, an unreasonable claim on my time and energy.

Even when she has a relatively small class, a schoolteacher has twenty-two great kids and four or five who cause trouble. As a principal with, say, sixteen classrooms in your school, you now have up to eighty kids who run your life in a not-so-good way. The principal gets to know these kids far too well. Not just one teacher's four or five, but every teacher's four or five. The fifteen percent who land in your office take at least ninety percent of the time you have available for kids. That whole first year at Miller, I sometimes knew what to do and did it, and other times had no idea. Sometimes I thought I knew, and still fumbled the situation. Fortunately, most of the teachers were good at managing even their most disruptive kids.

First at Miller and later at Brichta, I found a small minority of teachers with short tempers who could provoke trouble with their students, teachers who not only started power struggles but also escalated them and blamed the whole thing on the child. A couple of teachers I knew simply bored the kids into bad behavior. Every teacher has her limits, and many subtly give one child more of a chance and another less. You can sometimes catch a teacher or a playground monitor applying standards more strictly to any group that is "other" to them: boys, or children with disabilities or of a certain color.

Some teachers, new and inexperienced or older and burned out, give too many warnings without enforcing a clear limit. These teachers then snap and blame the children, who can't know when the line will stop moving. Instructors who merely "cover" the curriculum without generating purpose, engagement, and a sense of community miss their best chance to win the kids over to learning. Why should kids sit there and suffer no matter how boring or repetitive the lesson is?

Remember taking turns reading paragraphs in the social studies text and answering the questions at the end of the chapter? Can you even remember that teacher's name? Those teachers don't get why all the rules in the world don't keep bored and alienated kids from acting up. But, the more I "helped" a few teachers by taking the kids who were unwanted, uninspired, or restless into my office, the more I kept alive the illusion that it's all about the individual rotten kid.

Teachers who manage well use various combinations of learned strategies and instinct, of clear rules and wise exceptions. These teachers only called on me for the serious violations, the scary outbursts of the behaviorally disordered or mentally ill kids. In that first year at Miller, my ignorance left teachers who had the most difficult kids to struggle along as best they could. Early in my career, I learned to assign the weaker teachers a smaller share of the violent, the yet-to-be-diagnosed mentally ill, and the ones with belligerent parents. I make no claim that it was fair to burden the stronger teachers with more than their share.

I worked with the handful of teachers who didn't manage well in how to set up a classroom, how to choose relevant and motivating materials, how to design active and interesting lessons, and how to set limits and manage behavior without yelling and sending mixed signals. I also had teachers visit successful colleagues in our school or elsewhere. These efforts didn't always overcome defensiveness, laziness, or poor attitude. Even had I been so inclined, I couldn't have given some teachers enough back-up to stop them from complaining that no one was doing anything to make their students behave.

Today, 10:38 a.m.

The note in my pocket about Jenifer's sad day has brought me to her kindergarten classroom just as the kids are lining up for lunch. Mrs. Sorensen, the teacher, is a master at dealing with troubled children, and her patience usually extends far beyond mine. Jenifer is only the second-most troubled and troubling child in Mrs. Sorensen's class, because RaeLee is first. Today, I'm relieved that Jenifer, and not RaeLee, needs my attention. For one thing, Jenifer can't run as fast as RaeLee. But Jenifer is more likely to bite, kick, or hurl insults at the other kids. Her targets are usually too stunned to reciprocate, or even to defend themselves against her version of the drive-by.

Inside the classroom, three children crowd each other at the sink while another seventeen trail back from the hallway door in a single-file line. I have visited Mrs. Sorensen's room so many times this school year that the kids scarcely notice me. I don't see Jenifer right away, but Mrs. Sorensen signals me with her eyes to look under the table next to the sink. There I spy a tiny girl with dark blonde hair hunched among a tangle of table legs and pint-sized chairs. Because her chosen table clears the floor by eighteen inches, Jenifer can't sit upright. She turns her tear-streaked face in my direction for a moment and then looks away.

Jenifer is extra small from some combination of her mother's drug habit and having to beg the neighbors for food from the time she could walk. Child Protective Services has been working for two years to re-unite this scatter of single mom, Jenifer, and four-year-old twin boys, but the plans keep falling through. In the meantime, a woman old enough to be Jenifer's grandmother, maybe or maybe not a blood relative, takes care of Jenifer and the twins.

When the 10:40 bell signals the beginning of first lunch, Jenifer still huddles beneath the table. The kids in line shift and rock while Mrs. Sorensen looks from Jenifer to me and then to the line of waiting children. She can't leave Jenifer alone in the room, nor can she hold the other kids back from lunch.

By now infamous for this behavior, Jenifer stays somewhere she is supposed to leave or darts away, forcing Mrs. Sorensen to choose between this one child and the rest of the class. Remembering the couple of days in the past week that Mrs. Sorensen missed lunch to deal with RaeLee, I tell her that I'll stay with Jenifer, and say more loudly, hoping Jenifer will want to join them, "Why don't you go on to lunch now with the class." As the line of children heads out the door, I take three steps toward them as if that's what all of us are going to do.

When they are gone and Jenifer hasn't moved, I walk back toward her and say, "Let's walk together to the cafeteria."

Law and history entitle me to manage the movement and whereabouts of any child or adult on school grounds. In the years before Ricky's arrival at Brichta, I still imagined I could freely exercise this authority over children for their safety or for the safety of others. By my fourth year at Brichta, I was starting to encounter dislocational children, the ones who refused to go where they were told—as in, *you go to the office right now*—or who ran off campus in the middle of class.

By the late 1990s, these situations presented themselves at least two or three times a week. I could command, threaten, and beg, but would have no luck dislodging the stayer or talking the runner in from the edge of the playground. The public, the school district, and the parents count on us to have Somebody available not only to keep children safe, but to launch a search, to wait it out with the child who refuses to move from a spot in a classroom or hallway, to coax a child back from a far corner of the playground, or to sit on the floor next to the boy who has upended his chair and turned over his desk.

In just my last two years, on one day or another, we needed Somebody to change Down syndrome kindergartner Paula's diapers, Somebody to stay with mentally ill Holly while she panicked for 45 minutes in the hallway outside her classroom, and Somebody to follow "runner"

Vincent when his voices told him he needed to leave school grounds. At Brichta, this Somebody didn't exist except when I played the role of the mythical extra person. And if we actually had the several extra Somebodies, the tax-paying public would condemn us for being overstaffed.

Jenifer contorts her little body to peek out from under the table, then turns away and goes on ignoring me. Even if my only audience is a troubled five-year-old, I pretend I have all the time in the world, the grand illusion of the principalship. Moving slowly, I pull a couple of the chairs away from Jenifer's table, then lower my knees to the floor beside her and take hold of her nearest hand. I pull just enough to show I'm serious, but stop short of yanking or forcing. At least she doesn't jerk her hand away, doesn't totally resist.

Echoing my cautious pace, Jenifer at last starts to move out. It seems like a full minute, an eternity in school time, before she gets herself upright. She allows me to take her hand, but she leaves her own little paw slack in mine. As we move through the doorway, she stretches her other hand up to switch off the lights.

My hand is already starting to sweat in its limp clutch with Jenifer's. Before we get very far, we nearly trip over a straggler from another class who points at Jenifer and loudly asks, "What happened to her?"

"Honey, it's not your business," I say.

The boy in front of us dawdles his way forward, turning his head a couple of times to make sure we are not doing anything too interesting. Jenifer starts to snuffle and then to sob. She suddenly narrows her hand as if to pull it out of my grasp, to run ahead of me and around the corner. Since her wiry 37 pounds could hurt me if she resists being carried, I'll only pick her up as a last resort. A dramatic move like that wouldn't show Jenifer anything she doesn't already know and might not even satisfy my impatience.

1986–87, Miller School

That first year at Miller, hoping to make up for my rookie ignorance about student behavior, I started a new conversation. Around the time the school board had appointed me Miller's principal, I'd read a research article about *collegiality,* a term I had never heard before.[2] Without knowing how to pronounce this new word—hard g or soft g?—I knew at once that a power-and-control model of leadership would not provide the vitality I wanted for a school. Unless they were doing their jobs badly, I didn't want to control the daily work lives of individual teachers. But I did want them to talk with each other about what they did to help kids learn, and why they were doing it.

After the winter break, I found time to talk with the teachers one by one or in small groups around the lunch table. I talked about teaming up, collaborating, even sharing kids so that one teacher might work with a larger group while another teacher or two worked with smaller groups for a time each day. My first choice of words for this new thing was "planning together." I tried not to pitch it as some bold new initiative or even a change of direction.

Miller's budget, set by the district's formula, included no money that I could use to send teachers to conferences, workshops, or even staff planning meetings outside of work hours. I risked the teachers regarding my ideas as more work for them rather than as an exciting opportunity for teamwork. As they were deciding over that winter whether to leave or to stay when Miller downsized in the spring, I was afraid to push my new ideas too hard.

With the staff cuts coming up, I didn't conduct any straw polls or try to second-guess who would move on. No one staged any dramatic showdowns or drummed up a let's-all-leave movement. The day arrived for my scripted announcement about cutting seven teachers. I didn't sleep well the night before the formal notice, and when the time came, I read it straight out of the book: "Due to an enrollment reduction of approximately 190 students for next year, Miller will have seven fewer teaching positions available."

By the next day, exactly seven teachers asked me to sign their transfer papers. Four hoped to move to elementary schools closer to their homes. One wanted to try middle school, and another took a job with the new school just south of us. The seventh, a brilliant teacher in her twenties, used this occasion to tell me she'd become engaged to the man who taught sixth grade in the room next door, and they thought it best to work in separate schools. Focused on learning the game of principal, I had managed not to notice this romance. It dawned on me that the seven, and perhaps a few others, had bargained among themselves to make this work. I was going to miss some of these teachers, but I felt relieved. They did not *all* hate me.

CHAPTER 9
A FEW DROPS
OF BLOOD

Today, 10:44 a.m.

ONCE THE BOY AHEAD of us walks on, I say to Jenifer, "Come on, let's get you something to eat. What do you think of that?" In retrospect, a purely dumb question made of words I imagine a nicer principal, one who is endlessly patient, might use.

I equalize our heights by kneeling in front of her, but Jenifer looks down and to one side. She remains silent as she pulls away halfheartedly, but still doing that skinny-hand thing that threatens to disconnect us. Failure starts to shadow my wish to be further along in the episode, in this day.

With the hand that isn't holding hers, I steady myself on the low hallway table and stand up, glad that my skirt is long enough to give me cover. Jenifer only resists a little and then comes along a half-step behind my own slow pace, but anyone watching would have thought I was dragging her. We make it through the two sets of doors between us and the cafeteria.

Fifty feet ahead of us, an untidy line of children stretches out from the cafeteria doors. The fact that a couple of the kids are actually sitting against the wall tells me that this line is moving far too slowly and that the kids' usual eagerness for lunch has spiraled down to resignation and crankiness. In his #34 Lakers jersey, a boy at the end of the line darts across the hallway, spins around, runs back and leaps up to slam a spot on the wall above his starting point. Upon landing, he just misses a girl's feet.

We have a cafeteria-helper vacancy that has gone unfilled all year because in 2001's economy, no one wants these low-paying, part-time, no-benefits jobs. Food Services couldn't send a substitute today. The lunch line creeps along, and I can't blame the kids for growing twitchy as they wait. Other than at a funeral, when do adults line up silently, feet still, hands to ourselves, no cuts? Only in the odd alternate universe called school do we expect this behavior, where tradition descends from the monastery and the cloister. I remain hopeful that behavior in schools can find a middle ground between chaos and church. I can only articulate this so many times each day, though, and I need everyone's help.

When Jenifer and I start to enter the cafeteria, I see that I can't just release her into the noisy room. Going through the motions of including her in a decision I've already made, I bend down and say, "How about if we eat in my office?" Jenifer's scowl doesn't lighten, but I persist, pulling her to the cashier's table. There we edge in ahead of the impatient kids whose lunches are already behind schedule. The brown-eyed boy who should be next gives me a startled look when I cut in, but he doesn't say anything, and I don't explain.

I use my free hand to take a spoon and napkin from their metal bins and stuff them into the pocket of my jacket, then grab a carton of chocolate milk from the refrigerator box. As we reach the serving counter, the din of seventy-five children all talking at the same time forces me to shout across the glass panel. Before she starts making up an adult lunch tray, the cafeteria lady needs to know that I'm getting lunch only for Jenifer. Today's menu options are a hamburger or macaroni and cheese. When the lady asks Jenifer to point to one dish or the other, Jenifer's arms stay at her sides. Impatient, I point to the macaroni, comfort food for lots of kids, and I hope it will be for Jenifer.

The lady spoons a small portion of the cheesy macaroni into a section of the plastic tray and adds some carrot sticks and a cookie. She sees that I don't have an extra hand for the tray, and she sets it where I can add the chocolate milk, napkin, and spoon. I grasp it with the hand that is not holding Jenifer's and try to get us out of there as fast as I can. I'm not quick enough to dodge a hug around the waist from a first grade girl. This Jenifer business has put the lunch line behind by at least a full minute.

I hold the lunch tray above the heads of the swarm of kids in the corridor. We have advanced a few steps up the hallway when Jenifer's teacher walks toward us, headed in the opposite direction. Jenifer's hand in mine shifts from slight resistance to neutral, and she utters her first words of the entire episode: "Hi, Mrs. Sorensen."

"Hi, Jenifer. Have a good lunch," her teacher says back, and keeps on walking. I stay out of it entirely. Six months into this school year, Mrs. Sorensen is one of the longest-term stable adults Jenifer has known in her brief and uncertain life. As Jenifer and I continue on our way, her little hand actually grasps mine for a second, but just as quickly, her grip loosens again.

1989–91, Miller School

August of 1989 marked the first time in my life I had returned to any job for a fourth year. Three years at Miller had left me feeling confident about what I was doing. As I'd intended, I'd gotten the staff talking about teaching and learning and I was heading into a more mature phase of the work. Most of the teachers who had stayed after that first year were still with me and I had been able to hire replacements for a few who'd left.

As I moved into this fourth year and beyond, I found it easier to talk with parents. I was enforcing necessary discipline among the students and I'd earned positive evaluations from my supervisor. In 1991, the district appointed me to a statewide testing committee that would create alternatives to multiple-choice testing. We would develop new performance measures that assessed thinking, problem solving, and application of knowledge and skills to real-world questions. This seemed to signal continued progress of the kind I had counted on when I'd become an educator.

This was also the start of a bad period for my school district. Our Superintendent of Schools, Paul Houston, left for a job in California. Thoughtful and wise, Dr. Houston had been the only superintendent ever to visit me at school and talk with me about my work. I had little idea what to expect from his replacement. The new superintendent had arrived fresh from losing a job in a Midwestern city and seemed bent on avoiding pitfalls he had encountered there. He was tall and wore three-piece suits, a practice that kept him at more distance from his Tucson staff than I believe he ever knew. Then again, perhaps that was his intention.

In the spring of 1992, the school district decided to move a class for fifth and sixth graders with emotional disabilities into one of Miller's two empty classrooms.

I hoped that, with a little help, our teachers might welcome the ED kids and their teacher, as they had welcomed the small class for the hearing impaired that had been at Miller for years. I asked the district for some help in preparing the staff—and me—for this new ED class. My supervisor suggested that I contact the head of special education or one of her top assistants to come and discuss how best we could integrate this new class into our school. I called, and then called again. I was not able to get a special education administrator of any level to pay even a fifteen-minute visit to a faculty meeting—or to me as the receiving principal—before summer vacation arrived.

The brand-new, fresh-out-of-college teacher assigned to Miller's ED class by central office was bright, thoughtful, and enthusiastic. Even though I'd had no voice in hiring her, I liked her and found her full of good ideas for running her first-ever class. She wore her dark-brown hair in a ponytail, smiled easily, and stood just over five feet tall, about the same size as a couple of the boys who would be in her room. She and her two somewhat more experienced assistants would welcome ten boys and two girls. In the couple of days before the kids arrived, the new teacher and her assistants set up the desks, bookshelves, and other furniture. They drew up a point system to reward the kids for doing what they were supposed to be doing, with small prizes they could claim on Fridays if they had followed the rules during the week.

On the middle Monday of August, 1992, I crossed my fingers as the twelve children climbed down from the bus. To get on the ED class roster, these children had already been identified by their neighborhood schools as unmanageable in a regular classroom. For this, they had been relocated to Miller, another neighborhood school that had a room available, where they would have only each other as role models. The twelve students coming to Miller ranged in height from four feet to just over five feet. About half of them were what we called Anglo, with the other half a mix of Hispanic, African-American, and Native American.

Although not one of them came to us with a medical diagnosis beyond the usual attention deficit with hyperactivity, I knew that some of these children had been abused, while others showed early signs of mental illness. If the child was not mentally ill and still lived with some version of his biological family, one or both parents might be socially or emotionally unbalanced.

While the psychologists were able to distinguish kids whose disorder involved conscience-free aggression and disruption from the emotionally bruised and mentally ill, our school district chose to mix them in the same classrooms, against professional norms of best practice. This led to endless rounds of the budding criminals goading the borderline-psychotic, then gloating over their success at provoking eruptions. Now, with no help or special preparation, our job was to control everyone's behavior just enough to teach them some basic skills. School was never to be confused with therapy.

Some people imagine that all it takes to "control" a child's behavior is a stern glance or a limit clearly spoken, an authority figure walking tall, or a prize awarded upon the accumulation of good behavior points. If you are still in that camp, you have never spent a day with a mentally ill child.

My first mistake was putting the ED class in a room next to a door that opened directly to the east playground. This was the same door the kids would use to get to restrooms that, for some reason, also had doors that opened only to the schoolyard rather than to a hallway. Lacking experience with setting up a class for emotionally disabled children and lacking a supportive visit by anyone who knew more about it than I did, I had not stopped to consider what we'd do in an emergency.

Walking fast, I would need nearly a minute to reach that part of the building from the office, and a minute can be a very long time in these matters. If one of the teacher aides escorted two or three of the boys to the bathroom, the other nine or ten children stayed in the classroom with the teacher and the other assistant. Any arrival or departure sorely tempted these remaining children to shout, throw something, tip over a desk, or punch a classmate in the stomach.

From that first morning, I was on the phone twice a day with the director of the special education support office for our school. The director was one of the people I had begged for help in preparing for this new class, one who'd seemed to shrug at the apparent unimportance of my request. Much of the time, I found myself tensing my shoulders and sometimes forgetting to breathe.

I would have been completely out of luck with the kids' daring escapes, the turned-over desks, and the ruined lessons if it had not been for Nancy. Nancy was a gutsy support specialist who worked out of a district center like the one I'd supervised before I transferred to Miller. She had taught at Miller for a couple of years and had interned with me while getting her administrative certificate. When her boss continued to ignore my pleas for help, I called Nancy directly.

Every day for nearly two months, Nancy arrived at Miller in jeans and sneakers before the class bell rang. She helped me figure out how to move the ED class to a room nearer the office, one that had in fact been built to hold the smaller special needs classes. Now, Nancy and the teacher and I agreed that the smaller room would work much better than the more spacious room in which they'd started out. Once we'd moved the furniture, books, supplies, and then the students,

Nancy worked alongside the teacher to get the kids' behaviors in check enough that they could start to learn something.

Today, 10:51 a.m.

Still using both hands to keep Jenifer and her lunch tray headed toward my office, I notice a trail of bright red drops on the floor near Brichta's front doors. Blood. I pull Jenifer to one side so she doesn't step in it. I have to stop myself from somehow growing an extra hand and finding a rag to wipe up this new threat to health and safety. The custodians have a bleach spray we are supposed to use, or at least that's what they tell us in our annual blood safety updates. The mess will probably triple in size by the time Susie gets the custodian up here from the cafeteria, but I stop myself from taking care of it while I'm trying to get Jenifer settled.

Too often, this fixing reflex sidetracks me. Every moment of every day seems to carry this choice: fix or move forward, fix or move forward. I've never had the time to count up the accumulation of the unfixed, the unfinished, the unmet needs that clutter the road behind me. In these later years on the job, I struggle onward, trying to stare down the urgent when it is not important, but as often as not, I give in just to get one more thing out of the way.

Some days I take a break from the long-range planning, the microanalysis of data, or figuring out what to do about a struggling teacher or about the one who can teach well enough but is mean to the kids. Retreating from the action for a few hours can work as long as no one needing to be saved or repaired bursts into my space, and life at Brichta often runs smoothly enough to allow an occasional hunkered-down day. I answer e-mail, check the news on the internet, visit classes briefly and without much interest, deal with every little thing, but close my door at lunchtime.

At last inside my office, I let go of Jenifer's hand and lay her lunch tray on the round table. On her last visit, she spent an hour under this same table, refusing to play the game of talk-with-the-principal about why she'd kicked and hit Roman. I view her choice of chair over floor as progress. Now, she climbs aboard the one chair that has arms and pulls the tray toward her, where it sits near the edge of the table at her shoulder level.

Jenifer spoons up one macaroni noodle, places it in her mouth, and slowly chews. I pat her shoulder and am again shocked by how the bone sits right there under skin, no padding. "Let me know if you need any help," I offer.

With Jenifer semi-settled, I want to phone the mom who called about bad language in the talent show. As I start to press in the numbers, I hear Jenifer's soft voice. "Can you help me open my milk?"

I put the phone back in its cradle and take the half-pint carton from Jenifer's hand and open the flaps and then the spout. She tips the carton up just enough to pour a few drops of milk into her mouth, then sets it down carefully. Next, she spoons up another bite of the macaroni, chews, swallows, then takes another slow-motion mouthful, two noodles this time.

Though I feel grateful for this shred of connection, the morning's messages and notes still wait on my desk. I'll let Jenifer eat for a while, I rationalize. If I bother her with questions now, she might crawl under the table again, and then where will we be? On this Tuesday in the spring of my last year on the job, the odd dignity in Jenifer's resistance, the spot of control she asserts in an otherwise chaotic life, fascinates me.

Jenifer has eaten about half of the macaroni, has taken two mouse-bites from the cookie, and has given herself a chocolate milk mustache. She has placed the carrot sticks end to end, forming a line on the tabletop near her tray. Doing my bit to help her catch up with her peers in height and weight, I encourage or arm-twist, depending on your perspective. "That chocolate milk looks good. Do you want to take some more sips?"

She looks up at me but says nothing. She starts to reach for the carton, then stops, careful to remain in control of the situation. Jenifer looks at me again, then nibbles at the cookie. I don't push her to tackle the carrots that sit on the table surface. Thanks to the mucus, tears, and dirty hands of so many visitors, my table must by now be one of the most bacterially active spots on earth.

I switch my strategy: "Do you want to tell me what happened in class that got you upset?"

Jenifer whispers, "No."

OK, so I'll work at something else for a few minutes, use this fragment of time to check off another "do" item. My in-basket sits on top of a filing cabinet just outside the door to my office, as many steps from Susie's desk as from mine. Reaching toward it now, I nearly bump into Susie in the doorway.

Just then Jenifer's soft voice snags me back, and I ask Susie to wait a moment. Jenifer says, "Bret wouldn't let me wash my hands."

"What happened?" I ask.

She repeats the sentence again in a monotone, but a little louder, as if my moment of attention to Susie reflects either deafness or stupidity on my part. "Bret wouldn't let me wash my hands." This wouldn't amount to much for most kids, but for Jenifer it is too big for her to work around today, when she won't be seeing her mother after all.

Until she moved into foster care nine months ago, Jenifer didn't know that families had mealtimes, bedtimes, or any routines whatsoever. No one had ever shown her how or when to wash her hands. The fostering relative and Mrs. Sorensen have pushed and pulled Jenifer to perform this cleansing ritual before lunch, something she is now proud to do along with the other kids.

I say, "Oh, honey, I'm so sorry to hear that."

Still there, waiting while Jenifer tells me about Bret, Susie says, "You'll like the message I just put in your basket." Have I said two words to Susie yet today? I make brief and grateful eye contact with her.

CHAPTER 10
SO CRAZY LATER

1992–93, Miller School

SOMETHING CAN SEEM SO reasonable at the time and
so crazy later. Most Augusts, the district held a back-
to-school conference for administrators. We would
hear about any new rules or procedures and get re-
focused and motivated for the coming year. This year,
my seventh at Miller, the year the ED class arrived,
our new deputy superintendent had brought in a
motivational speaker from a university in the Midwest.
This semi-famous guest speaker had just published a
new book on leading with soul, spirit, stewardship,
emotional intelligence, or some other quality that in
our twenty-first century punishment culture would
be dismissed as "soft."

At the conference, this speaker reminded us to cultivate *relationship* as a primary focus of our jobs. He had moved and impressed me, had charged me up for my work at Miller that year. If the deputy had brought Professor So-and-So in for our back-to-school pep talk, I thought, maybe the deputy had a softer side that had escaped me, but one to which I could pitch my concern about the way the ED class had landed at Miller.

After several weeks of Nancy's help, I managed to set up a meeting with the deputy. Communication, I believed, would help us resolve this situation. I didn't intend to complain *that* the class had been sent to us. I intended to spotlight the *manner* in which it had been sent, without an ounce of communication or coordination. The bus transportation office, the kids' parents, and the Miller School staff had all been disregarded as plans were made. Why couldn't someone from central office come and help us figure out which room might work best, what backup we needed in case of emergency, what support a brand-new teacher might need, and how we could make sure that all our kids stayed safe?

I was determined to find a fix that might help us even now, several months in. Miller was not the only school where an extra room had been commandeered with little warning and no support, so I invited a few other principals who had gone through this to come along to the meeting. A second, less obvious issue also went with us.

While I was at Miller, and again while I was at Brichta, another school not far away received a class for gifted children at each grade level. Even then, low test scores could bring negative attention to a school. Required to test all children, the school who receives a concentration of special needs students from outside its boundaries will inevitably show lower scores than it would have without these additional children. Meanwhile, the school up the street, with its catch of gifted and talented from miles around, has no worries even though its neighborhood kids score below average.

The deputy superintendent kept us waiting about ten minutes past our appointment time before seating us around his long cherry-veneer conference table. This was the exact room in which, nearly fifteen years earlier, Dave had told me that researchers were full of shit. Now, a man I had not learned to trust sat at the head of the table. I sat to his right and my two colleagues sat across from me. The special education director and some of her staff faced us from the other end of the table. The bright sunlight coming through the window behind the deputy made it hard for us to read his facial expressions.

Not wanting to whine about a situation that was testing me more than anything since my first year as principal, I reframed my complaint as a set of suggestions. "Next time, we could really use some coaching before the class comes over, like how to choose which room the class should be in," I started out.

I finished with, "Even though this is school and not therapy, the emotionally disturbed kids need some kind of mental health person checking in on them more often than every two weeks."

As I offered each of my ideas, or one of my colleagues chimed in, the deputy wrote something on a piece of paper. He would look over at the special education director and say, "Can you do that?"

"Yes," she said, to every one of his questions.

In the middle of the meeting, the deputy had his secretary summon someone else to the meeting, and he asked us to stop our meeting until she arrived. Since we seemed to be taking a little break, I used the moment to thank the deputy for the motivational speaker he had brought in for the August meetings. Overtalking my point, I went on, "Some people think we can engineer these things, learning and teaching, but I think it's a lot more complex than that."

The deputy didn't exactly frown, but just as the sent-for administrator arrived and joined us at the table, the deputy said, "Of course we can engineer it. It's called *human* engineering."

I opened my mouth to protest, but managed to shut it and let the moment pass. I left the meeting buoyed by my apparent success in getting them to grant my appeal for advance planning, to assure me that things would be different for other schools that needed help.

None, absolutely none, of the promised help ever showed up.

Today, 11:15 a.m.

With Jenifer working her way noodle-by-noodle through the macaroni, I find once again that my six-foot phone cord doesn't reach far enough to let me sit with her at the round table. The rest of the civilized world has been using cordless phones for years. Is this beyond the district's budget, beyond their grasp of the job I am trying to do, or simply one more example of how we have to work less efficiently so the tax-paying public won't think they are pampering us?

Twisting in my desk chair to keep Jenifer in view, I punch in the phone number for the mom who's worried about the talent show. She starts right in. "There are some boys doing a rap thing right after my daughter's dance number, and my daughter says they're going to use a song by M and M or something like that. I've never heard of him. She says he uses bad language."

"Do you know the boys' names?" I ask.

"No. Sorry. I think my daughter knows at least one of them. I don't want to get anyone in trouble, but . . ."

I end the call shortly after that, with the promise that I'll check into it.

I hear this not wanting to get anyone in trouble four or five times a week, often about bad things that have already happened. Most of the time, getting someone in trouble is exactly what they do want, but they want me to be the enforcer, principal to the world. At least this mom turns out to be one of the friendly ones. Actually, most of them are.

Legends about difficult parents are based on the exception and not on most of the ones I knew across my fifteen years. I drop my shoulders and roll my head around a couple of times. I see that Jenifer has stopped eating and is looking over at me, so I say, "It sounds like you had a really tough time in class this morning. Are you feeling better now?"

Principals and teachers always want kids to say they're feeling better. It's the tiniest measurable increment of success and a "yes" gives you permission to move on to the next thing. Jenifer doesn't speak. Watching her, I realize that she has the same dark blonde hair and brown eyes that I had when I was her age. Through my own school years, I was one of the short kids, but not scrawny like she is. Jenifer and I live in parallel universes of nothing and everything, another reason for me to feel guilty that I want this whole thing to move along faster.

If I hurry now, maybe I can find the talent-show girl in the lunch line and I can get her to tell me who the alleged foul-mouthed rapper is. After that, I'll still have fifteen minutes to see Caleb and Ricky before fourth grade lunch. Is Jenifer ready to go back to class without falling apart? I lie a little and tell her that Karen would love to see her in the health office, the second time today I've presumed on Karen's warm heart and told this fib. Again silent, Jenifer picks up her lunch tray and follows me into the health office. She has relaxed out of her scowl, but her little face remains solemn.

I make it all the way to the cafeteria line without getting snagged sideways into anything else. The classes in this lunch run are just arriving, and they line up along the wall for the same wait the younger kids endured a while ago. So the talent-show girl won't be overheard snitching, I try to make this look like a chance encounter. I say, "I hear you've got a pretty wonderful dance number in the talent show. Are you right before that little kindergarten girl who's singing the Siamese cat song?"

This lets her say "No" and mention the name of the boy scheduled after her.

I hurry to get Caleb before his lunch bell sounds and start in while we walk toward my office. "How's it been going between you and Mitchell?"

Caleb glances up at me the way Mitchell did earlier, searching my face for further information. When I don't respond, Caleb says, "I told Greg I felt like kicking Mitchell's butt. Ricky heard me and said he'd help me. Greg has a big mouth."

Caleb's poker face is almost as good as mine, so I'm unprepared for the next thing he says. "Mitchell's going out with Cheralyn. I was going out with her, but we broke up last week."

Going out? Broke up? I stop my jaw from flapping open. The kids have explained that they don't actually go *out*, but they—fourth graders, lots of them—do talk to each other on the phone after school and call each other girlfriend and boyfriend. The girls fight a little more over romantic drama than the boys do, and the other kids focus endless gossip on these alpha couples.

As Caleb leaves, Susie tells me that the substitute teacher called on the intercom to ask me to speak to the kids before they go to lunch in a few minutes. She mentions paper airplanes flying at unpredictable intervals. The bogus orchestra departure was not the only distraction. I go.

This disorderly class has seen so much of me this year that only a few kids seem curious about why I show up just now. In one of his pinball moods, Bradley ricochets off a table, the reading center sofa, another boy's back, and the edge of the counter next to the drinking fountain. After baseball-sliding in the general direction of his desk, he flips the top up and down three times before pulling out his chair and sitting down.

The substitute stands off to my left while I center myself in front of the room. I hold up my hand in a "give me five" move that I encouraged the regular teacher of this class to use. The kids surprise me by quieting and actually looking at me and putting their hands up to mirror my open palm. Hoping that I'm not coming across as sappy, I tell them to show today's guest teacher that our school is the best in the West. Curbing my impulse to lecture, I look over at the substitute and say loudly enough for everyone to hear, "I'll be around if you need me. Just call the office."

Next, I stop in Karen's office and ask Jenifer if she is "ready," that same teacherish question I put to Patrick a while ago when he was in the office for singing, the question that has only one right answer. Jenifer nods yes and gets up from her chair. I find a second grader who seems happy enough to walk her back to Mrs. Sorensen's room.

The clock shows 11:41 when I put my store-bought frozen enchiladas into the microwave that sits on my office shelf. I set the dial for five minutes and then open my newspaper to the comics page and take a few bites out of my apple. Schoolmaster folklore has long held that at the school's lunchtime I should simultaneously patrol the cafeteria, walk the playground, and sit in my office, available for drop-in visits from teachers, kids, parents, and pretty much anyone else. We must never appear too busy to take on the needs of the next teacher, child, parent, salesperson, or central office maintenance worker.

I have just started on the enchiladas and the comics when Mary knocks at my door.

"Sorry," she says. "I know you're trying to eat. There's a man here who wants to see you." I give her a puzzled look, and she says, "He's Rosie's grandfather." I have never met this man, in fact didn't know he existed.

"OK," I say to Mary, and fold up my newspaper and hide the partially eaten apple and the container of enchiladas inside the microwave.

1993–94, Moving

After seven years, I felt confident that I'd learned the job of principal at Miller. I had accomplished what I'd set out to do. Kids learned in active classrooms. Teachers were not afraid to try new approaches, and they talked with each other about teaching and learning. The Miller teachers and I could discuss our work as a group and arrive at decisions in which everyone had a voice.

At the same time, I noticed that I was holding back from telling teachers what to do. When I should have been pushing someone to improve, or to think in new ways about what they were doing, I stayed quiet. Had I just gotten too comfortable with them? I realized that Miller needed a change and that I did too. The school district announced plans for a new school a few miles from my home, and they were going to hire a principal early enough to help plan the school, from choosing carpet colors to hiring the staff. I wanted to do this. When the transfer opportunities were posted after the winter break, I put the new school at the top of my list.

By mid-February, I found that one of my favorite colleagues had been appointed to the new school. My transfer would be to Brichta. A few weeks after my new assignment was announced, my supervisor set up an after-school meeting to introduce me to the Brichta teachers. Sitting together in the school library, we ate cookies and drank red punch out of Styrofoam cups. They all told me their names, and I said that I was happy to be coming to Brichta and that I looked forward to getting to know them.

I wondered what they liked most about Brichta, what they might want to see changed, and what they wished for me to know about them. Not wanting to put individuals on the spot during this very superficial meeting, I handed out sheets of paper on which I'd listed a few questions. Most of the sheets came back to me with only the first question addressed, and addressed in an almost uniform manner, "I like how we all get along here." I had no idea I'd asked them to engage in risky behavior.

CHAPTER 11

READY OR NOT

1953, Tucson

DURING MY EARLY WEEKS OF first grade at Cragin
Elementary, I learned to put up with the many times
each day that my teacher called me Carolyn. Other
things seemed to go well enough, and after a while I
stopped protesting. I buddied up quickly with two of
the girls and enjoyed the attention of a few of the boys.

Even before she sat us down for the reading readi-
ness test a couple of weeks into the school year, Mrs.
Aldrich let me use the advanced first-grade reader,
the hardcover *Our New Friends*, instead of the three
soft-covered pre-primers over which the other kids
labored. It only took me a few pages to find that Dick
and Jane and Sally spoke in a way that sounded funny

to me after the comics and library books I had been reading.

One morning, Mrs. Aldrich pushed our low tables as far apart from one another as they would go. She told us to scoot our chairs inches this way or that so we wouldn't be tempted to peek at our neighbor's paper. By this time, most of us had figured out that, in school, "neighbor" meant the kid sitting next to us and not the family in the house next door to ours. After we had moved ourselves around to her satisfaction, Mrs. Aldrich gave each of us a stapled sheaf of papers and said we'd use this booklet to "play some games."

Jeffrey, the tallest and most mature boy in the class, got to hand out the fat eraserless pencils. Mrs. Aldrich said to fold our hands on the front covers of our booklets and listen to her directions.

Since we were not supposed to be able to read yet, Mrs. Aldrich told us to "look at the pictures." She would say "draw a circle around the boat" and then she waited while we drew a circle around the black-line image of a rowboat. In the section that had rows of three pictures, I had no trouble penciling a circle around the picture that matched each word she pronounced.

We had made our way through ten or fifteen of these when we came to a row that showed a line drawing of a waterfall, then a rough cartoon of an Indian chief in feathered headdress, and finally a sketch of a train locomotive. I waited for Mrs. Aldrich to say the word.

"*Injun*," she pronounced

I sat straight up in my chair. *Huh?* I wasn't sure what to do. When the kids had asked Mrs. Aldrich to repeat some of the words for earlier items, I had been impatient, had regarded my classmates as babies. But my teacher had been willing to say the word over again for the other kids, so I raised my hand and asked her to say this one again.

Smiling at me, she repeated in a louder voice than usual, "**Injun**."

I had to think fast. I had heard people say "Injun" for Indian, but I had never heard anyone say it for *engine*. My dad had told me that "Injun" was not the right way to say Indian even if people said it that way in the movies, that an Indian might feel insulted if you called him that. The other kids were marking their answers. Without an eraser, I had one chance, so I drew a less-than-committed circle around the picture of the chief. I'll never know which picture my teacher meant.

1994, Miller School

The custodian came to my office one spring day just after lunch to tell me he'd spotted a swarm of bees hugging a tree in the central courtyard. The district's safety office had blitzed us with dos and don'ts for schoolyard invasions of Africanized bees, or what the media liked to call "killer bees." The interbreeding of these aggressive bees with our local honeybees was well underway.

Faced with my first bee crisis, I put out an all-call on the intercom telling everyone in the building to close windows and doors. Next, while I jogged a big circle around the building to round up any kids or teachers who were outside, my secretary called the Sheriff's office, School Safety, and our assistant superintendent.

Just as I got back to the office, two boys ran out the door of the ED classroom and headed toward the bee tree. I shouted at them to stop, but Joseph and Malcolm climbed into the tree well and started pitching rocks at the swarm, yelling *"Kil-ler bees! Kil-ler bees!"*

Their teacher and I walked slowly toward the boys and the bees until we were about forty feet away. Not wanting to stress the situation further, the teacher and I took turns asking the boys nicely, schoolmarmishly, to stop throwing rocks and get away from the tree. They didn't even glance in our direction. We edged a little closer and continued begging. After we'd been at this for about five minutes, Sheriff's Deputy Martinez ran into the courtyard from the parking lot. He planted himself between us and the boys and hollered as loud as he could, *"Get back inside right now."*

As Joseph and Malcolm slunk toward the office door, Deputy Martinez rattled his handcuffs and announced, *"You are under arrest."*

Before he wound down, he informed them that they had *no right* to make the bees mad and try to get them to sting everyone at school. He finished the loud part with, "*I don't care if your parents ever come to get you out of juvie.*"

Meanwhile, the bee-removal specialist arrived and went right to work. I thought he'd actually *remove* the bees, make them vanish from the scene altogether. I hadn't thought at all about whether the bees would live or die, but had just pictured them gone. Instead, hundreds of them littered the floor of the courtyard, some still squirming. Our very unhappy custodian showed up at my elbow and asked, "Am I supposed to use a broom?" I grimaced and suggested he try a shovel.

Miller and I were not finished yet. By the last day of school, most of the books and supplies had been put away for the summer. The kids would not return until August, and after a week of closing school and packing up my office, I would not return to Miller at all. On that last day, the chalkboards in Miller's ED classroom contained only some recreational drawing and, in the corner of one board, a few semi-erased attempts at writing "fuck" without getting caught.

Gideon and the five or six other boys who'd be leaving for middle school swaggered to and from the drinking fountain and play-fought around the room. On this last day, their teacher tolerated some of this, but she and her two assistants stayed alert for trouble.

That Thursday was also Gideon's twelfth birthday. The teacher had baked a cake for him, chocolate-iced with "Happy Birthday Gideon" in big blue letters.

Later, his teacher would tell me that during the morning, Gideon had been fiddling with an out-of-season red wool scarf, winding it around his arm, taking it off, winding it again. In his two years at Miller, we had seen Gideon arrive at school some days with a smirky curve of the mouth and with his head cocked to one side, like a sleepwalker with a nasty edge. On those days, Gideon cackled instead of talked, pushed over tables, grabbed other kids around the throat, put his mouth up close to his teacher's face and said things she couldn't understand. The great-grandmother who was raising Gideon told me that weekly church didn't seem to be doing him any good. She said she couldn't hold on much longer and might have to give him up.

I had spent a year and a half catching Gideon on his good days, chatting about this or that, and inviting him along on work projects. He helped me box up old books or sort out the art closet. I had singled out this one needy kid for attention, imagining that my help could make some kind of difference, put him on the road to success, keep him out of jail, *repair* him. He seemed to enjoy these times and would talk to me about going with his great-grandmother to church, playing with his cousins on weekends, or how the man who lived next door to him had been arrested and taken to jail.

On that last day, I was visiting classrooms to say goodbye. A second grader had just offered me a cookie when I heard a ping from the intercom, the sound that let us know something was about to follow. My secretary's voice said, "Dr. Tompkins, please come to the office for a message."

I had just stepped into the corridor when Gideon burst in through one of the courtyard doors twenty yards in front of me. Lex, the teaching assistant, followed right behind him but didn't catch up to apprehend him. Holding one end of the red scarf above his head, Gideon walked as fast as he could in a crouching position, keeping the kind of low profile you might use for dodging bullets. Lex made eye contact with me and stayed back a little to avoid turning this into a chase. Seeing me ahead of him, Gideon hesitated, then waved the red scarf in a circle around his body and made a sudden left turn into another hallway.

I didn't want to run after Gideon. These are the times when you don't have time to think, just to react and hope that no one gets hurt. Lex and I watched Gideon pass the four classrooms across from the library and turn left at the next corner. From there, he poked his head back out to look at us a couple of times. I signaled to Lex to cut through the library to the hallway where Gideon waited while I kept walking toward the corner where he had taken cover.

Pretending that this was somehow normal, I called out "Happy birthday! Why don't you show me your scarf?" I wanted to avoid a scene like the one we'd had the previous Friday, one of his glassy-eyed days, when he'd run through the hallways opening doors and shouting curses into each room.

Now he stayed quiet, but dangled one hand around the corner to signal his location. To distract Gideon from Lex's detour through the library, I slapped the rubber soles of my shoes against the floor as I walked toward him. Just before I reached the turn in the white-tiled wall, Gideon drew his hand back, but I didn't hear him run away. I started thinking he must want to be captured. Just then, a scarf-wrapped fist grazed my left shoulder and connected hard with my lower jaw. My head tilted back and to one side. In the same second, Lex grabbed Gideon from behind and pinned his arms to his sides.

Gideon looked down and cackled but didn't pull away from Lex. I unwound the scarf from his arm. I didn't know what to say. The blow had shocked more than hurt me. *Shit*, I thought, I can't have him *arrested*, charge him with assault, on his last day of elementary school. *My* last day at Miller. I wanted to yell at Gideon for ruining my last afternoon, for not being sane, for not allowing me to repair him. My face started to feel numb from the effort of holding in my frustration and anger.

Lex and I didn't have a plan, but getting Gideon back to his room seemed like a start. Maybe we could get going on the birthday even if the party wasn't supposed to start for another half hour. Gideon let us walk him across the courtyard toward his classroom. He laughed a couple of times at something we weren't in on. When we walked in, his teacher gave Gideon a warm smile and offered him the new beginning that might help get us through this day. "Oh, good, you're back. Now we can celebrate your birthday."

But Gideon moved suddenly to the table holding the party food and, with his forearm, swept the birthday cake off the table. Big chunks of dark brown cake spread across the floor. We all froze. Not a one of us, no adult and no child in the room, had ever imagined someone doing this to his own birthday cake. We stayed quiet while the other teaching assistant angled the wastebasket toward the floor and used a piece of cardboard to scoop the hunks and crumbs into it. She ran water on some paper towels and scrubbed at the frosting that stuck to the carpet. I didn't wait to see what happened next.

I stepped into the little hallway that connected the classroom to the office and stood alone where no one could see me as tears threatened. *Because I've failed to mend him, to patch him up, to fulfill the principal's obligation to repair every student, no matter what it takes.*

The next time I would remember this incident was 2004, ten years after it happened and three years after I retired.

Part 2
Waist Deep

Around the time I applied for the transfer that took me from Miller to Brichta, I dreamt that I was on a journey to an indistinct and unfamiliar destination. In the company of both friends and strangers, loaded down with equipment, I walked for some time across a barren landscape that was less like my native desert than some sharp-edged mythic terrain.

Setting up camp on the shore of a lake at the end of the first day, I looked back in the direction from which we'd come, hoping to see where we'd begun. Instead, I found that jagged mountains extended upward from the water, obscuring the place from which we'd set out that morning.

I unfolded a map and found myself looking at a diagram that revealed with great clarity the impossibility of retracing our path. The map showed that this lake, these high mountains, blocked the return. There was no way back.

CHAPTER 12
ROSIE'S GRANDFATHER

Today, 11:40 a.m.

THE STOCKY AND GRAY-HAIRED man waiting for me wears clean blue work clothes. We shake hands, and I invite him to take a seat at my round table. After I shut my office door behind us, Rosie's grandfather says "I'm sorry to bother you, but I don't know what else to do. My wife and I are worried about Rosie."

He reminds me that his family is part of the Tohono O'odham nation, whose homeland spreads to the south and west of Tucson and across the border into Mexico. "We live out by the mission," he tells me, "but my daughter wanted to live closer to town."

Rosie and her mother have lived in the apartment complex across the ravine since October. As long as we have known them, they haven't had a phone. Rosie stays quiet in class and doesn't invite trouble. During the past month, she has spoken even less than usual, perking up only during her weekly half hour with a volunteer reading tutor. About a week ago, Rosie's teacher told me that Rosie's mother lost her job at the tribe's tobacco shop because she couldn't afford to get her car fixed and has no other transportation.

I tell her grandfather that we've been worried about Rosie, too. That remark puts me on the verge of breaking the law. I'm not supposed to discuss students' lives with grandparents who are not the children's legal guardians.

He pauses, then blurts, "It's about my daughter, Rosie's mom. I need for you to report her." Before I can ask what he means, he says, "We're pretty sure she leaves Rosie alone all night. I go to her place after I get off work at 9:00. I go three, four times a week. She hasn't been there even once."

Her grandfather stops, looks first at the floor, then at the ceiling, before he goes on. "Rosie makes excuses for her mother, but I know Helen's not coming home. I don't think she's buying food for Rosie. Maybe she has a new boyfriend." He looks slightly off to one side as he speaks.

Helen's car did not exactly break down, he tells me, but suffers from the theft of two of its wheels about a month ago. That night, Helen left the car—with Rosie in it—parked behind a bar and then got into another car with a man and drove off. Already shivering in the February night, Rosie couldn't fall asleep. When Rosie saw the bar patrons departing at closing time, she got up the courage to slip inside and ask the bartender for help. The bartender called the police, and an officer took Rosie home and dropped her off even though her mom was not there.

"My wife and I want Rosie to come live with us, but . . ." her grandfather trails off.

In my school district's cultural diversity classes, I've learned that the politics of his people make it nearly impossible for him to put his nose into his daughter's business. I also have some idea of the damage the peaceful Tohono O'odham Nation has sustained in their encounter with urban America over the past century. That little bit of understanding makes this visit both touch and astonish me. His desperate sharing of personal pain outside the family, outside the tribe, tells me he has tried everything he can think of within those customary boundaries. Only unbearable worry would have driven him to see me, an unknown white principal, about this.

Rosie's grandfather tells me that he's worked cleaning a state office building since 1985, two years after getting sober. "I took my daughter to some meetings, AA, but she doesn't stay on the wagon. It runs in families, you know." He speaks about this for another minute, then his volume goes down a notch as he says, "Please—don't tell them I came."

It's almost noon when he rises from my table to leave for work. I ask him to sign a form for Rosie to "shop" at the district's used-clothing warehouse even though I know that the rules say only Rosie's mother can give permission. With a signature on the form, Rosie can rummage through racks of donated shirts, shorts, and jeans for a few items that fit and that won't embarrass her. We've sent this form home twice since mid-February with no response. I count on the Clothing Bank not to catch the wrong signature. Lots of kids have last names different from their parents. Rosie's grandfather shakes my hand again as he leaves.

1994, Brichta School

In the 1969 classic work of ethnography, *The Man in the Principal's Office*,[3] an actual Oregon principal with the pseudonym Ed Bell spent a leisurely ten-hour workday doing things that would have occupied an hour and a half of my own day at school. Nowhere in that ethnographic study did Mr. Bell encounter children in foster care or parents suspected of using drugs. He conducted no investigations in which anyone's due process rights had to be observed. The student who worried Mr. Bell the most arrived at school somewhat unkempt, perhaps slightly neglected.

At 8:15 on my first morning at Brichta, a set of parents turned up demanding that I move their child from the class she'd been assigned to for this year. They wanted a different teacher, one that I was finding out had a better reputation than her colleague down the hall. I knew enough that first day to tell them that I can't give one teacher more kids than the other second grade teacher has. We want every child to learn in the smallest class possible.

What I didn't go on to explain in detail was something I'd learned at Miller: The whole staff knows which teacher gets requested the most, but it's an issue fraught with workplace politics and sensitivities. If you overload the better teacher, she can get resentful and say she doesn't have time to help the less-able teacher next door, the one with the smaller but very unruly class.

Without knowing the teachers or the parents on that first day at Brichta, I did know that when you have fifty second-graders, you can't give one teacher thirty-five kids and the other fifteen. I wanted to get along with parents, in fact had made good progress in that direction at Miller, but if I'd moved the girl to the other class, how would the Brichta teachers believe that I respected *them*?

I'd first met Margaret, the principal I replaced at Brichta, seventeen years earlier, on the day I'd started work as a program evaluator. Our paths had crossed often since then. Now, I found out that two of her grandchildren were enrolled in our upper grades. It turned out that many mornings, Margaret drove them to school and walked them inside, where excited Brichta students that I hadn't yet met ran up and hugged her. On these visits, Margaret also threw her arms around teachers whose names I was just learning, and she chatted with them in the hallways before class. When I witnessed these reunions, I'd slow down, sometimes even turn around and walk back the other way. I started to see that my new school was more different from Miller than I'd expected, and that I was a different principal from the one Brichta was used to.

I decided that I needed to explain myself, to help my new staff see who I was and not just who I wasn't. This was only partly personal. I wanted them to understand how I hoped to work with them, to do our jobs together. In one of our first faculty meetings, sitting in a ragged circle around tables in the school library, the teachers listened politely while I laid out my platform. Much as I had told the Miller teachers eight years earlier, I said that I hoped we could discuss our work as *colleagues*. A little after that, I added, "I don't believe that everyone has to teach the same way."

At Miller, I had known that principals were supposed to protect the teachers from the nonstop—and sometimes outlandish—central office demands, the kinds of demands I might have made when I'd worked downtown. Now, in that first Brichta staff meeting, I went on to say, "Mothering just isn't my style. I don't want to parent you. You're all adults. You're all professionals." It didn't cross my mind that day that some teachers regarded the principal's protection as *parental*, and they had just heard me say I would not *parent* them. One more time when I was thinking *role* and they were thinking *relationship*.

I started to tell them they shouldn't expect hugs from me, that I just wasn't a teddy bear, but I stopped myself. I didn't know if they'd be relieved or disappointed, and besides, watching Margaret bring her grandchildren to school, I hadn't sorted out my own feelings about this.

I moved on to deny a story that had run through the staff. A teacher who'd been out one day told others that I'd grilled her about her illness, and that I'd snooped into her business. Recalling no such thing, and still proud of how I had always honored the Miller teachers' rights to take sick or personal time, I felt hurt and annoyed. I vaguely recalled one 5:30 a.m. phone call that might account for this. I must have said something like "What's wrong?" or "Do you think it'll be more than one day?" or "I hope you feel better tomorrow."

The Brichta teachers and I had just met. Why were we already wrangling over this? As far as I could see, these teachers were as strong and mature as the Miller faculty had been. In the meeting that day, I said I was sorry if I'd offended someone by asking too much, and that I would be more careful. A week or so after the meeting, a teacher came to see me. She said, "When you told us you wouldn't ask about why we're taking leave, I got the idea that maybe you don't care about us. It didn't feel right." In this starting over, after all those years of easy give-and-take at Miller, every word I spoke now seemed projected on the wall in three-foot-high letters. Even a tiny detail of our lives together, and how I handled it, could threaten this new relationship.

Today, 12:15 p.m.

After I hang up from calling the child abuse hotline about Rosie—and receiving no promise that they will investigate—I open an envelope that landed in my basket while Jenifer was eating lunch. It is from a first grade teacher, and it holds a form she was supposed to fill out and bring to her evaluation conference last week, a list of her professional growth goals for the coming year. When she didn't bring it to our meeting, I asked her to get it to me as soon as possible. But the form I take out of the envelope now is blank and has a yellow sticky note attached.

> I can't do this so far ahead. How am I
> supposed to know what I'll do for prof.
> growth next year? Every time I set these
> goals the district comes up with some new
> thing they want us to do and that takes
> all our time.

I completely agree with her protest, yet her refusal to play the game annoys me a little. Year after year, we all experience whiplash as the school district sets new priorities before we've had time to absorb the last ones. I hold the hoops—district, state, and federal—through which teachers have to jump, and I police the deadlines for these even when I find no purpose in the undertaking. I feel pretty sure that the teachers see me as the rule-following, decree-enforcing boss who conspires in the stream of demands.

Out in the other world, the world of my colleagues and my bosses, I am the one putting the sticky note on the blank goals sheet, objecting to the domination of form over function, the ascendancy of nonsense. Even before I received the teacher's note, I had made her particular point to more than one of my bosses in front of scores of my colleagues. I waved my hand in the air at meetings, asked if this year's new initiative was now more important than last year's new initiative, the one that had just finished its pilot season, the one that was barely understood and barely underway.

1994, Brichta School

Even with the consternation I created in that first faculty meeting with my no-parenting pronouncement, life at Brichta flowed forward. The schedule, bells, lessons, recess, and lunch were the easy part. Whatever doubts some of them had about me, the teachers were in their classrooms doing their jobs.

The next layer of busy-ness was the unscheduled but regular stuff that any principal deals with: kids getting in trouble, parents popping in, the ping-pong of paperwork between school and downtown.

One Monday morning in that first month of school, the office manager told me that I had a phone call from the police. The officer asked if I knew that a boy had been caught skateboarding on the roof. I hesitated long enough for the officer to add, "Yesterday."

A neighbor had reported it, saying that she had more than once seen the boy swooping around Brichta's slightly pitched roof on a Saturday or Sunday. I found that the skater used to attend Brichta, but was now home-schooled.

Before we hung up, the officer asked if I wished to file a complaint. Even though it had happened on Sunday, and nothing, including the skater himself, was obviously damaged, I wanted this to be on the record somewhere, so I said yes. But I started to worry. Was it somehow the school's fault—*my* fault—that a skater and his board had been able to get up onto the roof? I took a slow walk around the outside of the building and found that a determined child *could* scale the walls in a couple of places and get a grip on the roof's edge, then pull himself up or get a boost from a friend.

When Brichta's budget showed up in mid-September, I flipped through the pages of green-lined computer paper to see what was left for learning materials like games, software, and extra books. I saw that Margaret had done some ordering in this category, but had left me around $2000. *Hooray.* At Miller, I'd always divided the money equally among the teachers and suggested that they group into twos or threes to purchase materials together and then share them. This was one of the ways I got them talking with each other about teaching. Most of them took my suggestion and no one ever complained about my method.

Accustomed to tight budgets, teachers and principals are always poised to grab at every little bit of money. For years, I had watched each crayon, pencil, and sheet of paper creep up in price. On top of that, money I had hoarded for second semester would get yanked back in March by central office. And, like siblings, people in schools notice who gets more and who, less.

Now, in my first month at Brichta, I divided up the money as I had at Miller, $120 for regular classes and half that for the smaller special education classes. I suggested that the teachers group into twos and threes. Most of them just stayed quiet and turned in their lists by the deadline. Only a few worked with colleagues. Two or three mentioned that this was the first time in years they'd gotten a slice of the learning materials budget. The office manager typed up the orders and mailed them in. I thought I'd had a modest success with my share-the-resources approach.

Chapter 13
Money Trouble

Today, 12:19 p.m.

It's the counselor's turn to run lunch detention today, and I find Ricky just leaving her office to go back to class after lunch. This time, he's right where he's supposed to be. He follows me back to my office and we sit across from each other at my round table. I lean back and relax a little when I ask him if something is going on between Mitchell and Caleb

I halfway expect Ricky to start on one of his usual sidetracks, like the one that goes, "My dad thinks you guys call him too much. He's afraid he might lose his job." Instead, Ricky fiddles with a pencil on the table and doesn't look at me as he says, "Marcia left."

My mouth forms an O at this mention of his dad's girlfriend, the one who has lived with them ever since I've known Ricky. He looks up at me and goes on. "My dad dumped her. Her kids were bringing too many friends over and they were eating all our food." Marcia's two teenagers crowd Ricky's apartment every other weekend. Ricky's story is flimsy, but seems to make sense to him. It's not my place to probe for details. Is Ricky upset or relieved? What am I going to do without Marcia? She has been our lifeline for whole seasons while Ricky's dad finished his courses and started working.

Now Ricky sits up straight in his chair, folds his hands on the tabletop, and puts on the face of an earnest little adult. He somehow manages to double the size of his hazel eyes. "It sure is quieter around the 'partment," he says. "We turn off the TV during dinner now."

I waver between amusement at his expression and alarm over his falling-apart family, but I reveal neither. I can't tell if Ricky is covering up, hoping to show me that the arrivals and departures of significant adults in his life are no big deal. Just because I could count on Marcia doesn't mean that Ricky could. And he's never given up hope about the woman he calls "my real mom." I have reached the point in this career where the Rickys, with their untidy lives and their school struggles, make more sense to me than I could have imagined in my early years back at Miller.

We shift back to the question I've asked him about Caleb and Mitchell. Ricky puffs up: "I was gonna try to get 'em to make peace. If I didn't have lunch detention today, I was gonna try to talk 'em out of it."

We go on a little, and Ricky tells me his version of the boys' competition over Cheralyn. After a bit, he deals. "Will you call my dad and tell him I *didn't* get into a fight?"

I deal too: "I'll call him tomorrow if there's no fight between now and then."

He grins and I grin back. We are old hands at this. Now that he is almost eleven, Ricky accepts my hugs only rarely, and I resist the urge.

1994, Brichta School

During the next six weeks, after we'd sent in the orders for teaching materials, one person or another would make an offhand comment about "the money." I wasn't sure what they were talking about. How could dividing the money into equal shares be controversial? Then one teacher hinted that my way of splitting up the money might have left some people feeling shortchanged, but she wouldn't name the people who might feel that way. She made these remarks during a conversation in which she'd seemed cordial, a conversation I'd regarded as friendly.

While the matter of "the money" still simmered, a core group of the staff, the veteran teachers, seemed to relax when they realized I wasn't going to force them to give up practices that had worked well for them. When I dropped by their classrooms, they seemed easygoing and just kept on teaching, with no dramatic pauses or greetings. They didn't ask questions that barely disguised complaints about things I was doing differently from Margaret. I was their fourth new principal in ten years, and they might outlast me, but in the meantime, they had a job to do.

When October was ending and the buzz about the money refused to die, I remembered how one of these veteran teachers had wrinkled her forehead and bitten her lip when the money topic had come up. She'd started to say something, and then left it at, "Never mind." Over the next month or so, I praised a special science program she was doing with her class and I complimented how she handled a touchy issue with a parent. I noticed that she smiled more when we ran into each other around the building, and that she said "Hi. How are you?" when she saw me at the start of the day.

I asked this teacher if we could talk after school. Since asking a teacher to talk after school can worry even the successful and confident, I said, "I need your advice on something." When I walked into her classroom later that day, her smile encouraged me to press on.

"I've been wondering about something," I started, not exactly sure how to say the next part. "There's a bunch of stuff about Brichta that I don't think I understood very well when I started. I probably still don't. Something about the money for materials seems to still be a problem."

Before I could go on, she cut me off. "Don't worry. It's OK."

But I needed more, so I asked, "Worry? What shouldn't I worry about?"

"They'll get over it."

"Over what?" I pushed.

"That they didn't get more."

"More than what? I only had $120 for each of you." This wasn't making sense to me.

"I'm just figuring you out. You're different from Margaret," she said, referring to my predecessor.

"How did Margaret do it?" I asked.

"I probably shouldn't say this, but I think she saved some of the money back for the ones who helped her with more stuff around school, so when we asked for something we got it. Nobody really knew how much anybody else got, but she usually had some money for me when I wanted something."

I thought about the two or three who'd said they hadn't received much money for extra materials, and I thought about the ones who had expected more. This second group overlapped with the group of veterans who had otherwise settled down and welcomed me into their classrooms. This didn't so much indicate that they trusted me as that they'd been through this before, this shuffle of leadership, and they had business to attend to.

No teacher should start out trusting a new principal, or even an old one. We are always going to let teachers down in one way or another. We can let them down inadvertently or in full knowledge, or somewhere in between. Any one of us will only earn trust in some categories of our work, and sometimes these categories are sufficient to get us forgiven for the parts where we're not so good. At Miller, I had gained the trust and respect of the teachers in areas related to shared decision-making and autonomy in the classroom, but how would the Brichta teachers know this? If they knew it, would these same categories be important to them?

I was naive not only in thinking these understandings would have reached from Miller to Brichta, but also in failing to find out what my new group cared most about. I was full-speed-ahead with democratic practice, and remained insensitive to how much the Brichta staff prized personal relationship. I had not cultivated that at Miller, had just practiced it a little with a few teachers who'd gone through divorces, illnesses, or legal troubles that they had felt moved to talk to me about.

I still don't know for sure how Margaret handed out the money for supplies and materials. Even if I had known back then, I think I'd still have done it my way. Not making an even division of the money would have gone against my core values. In a school, the better teachers shouldn't get richer at the expense of the ones who need more help. But I regret that I missed noticing how many of the Brichta teachers were still waiting for a sign that I cared, with some still hoping to be singled out for special recognition, as they had been before.

Today, 12:30 p.m.

When I walk out with Ricky, I find my Student Council officers waiting. These sweet children want my approval for some school spirit days, events that will involve goofy dress or behavior, like Backwards Day or Twins Day, with parades around the basketball court. They'll ask some PTO parents to judge costumes or performances, and they'll hand out small prizes.

I hate contests like this, but I don't tell them. Nurturing their leadership is more important than how I feel about these school-day frivolities. It takes us just under ten minutes to make a few adjustments in their proposal and to put dates on the master calendar. I shake hands with both of them as they leave. The time I spend in this meeting hardly counts against the minutes and hours I spend sorting out trouble.

I remember that I need to see my talent-show rapper and I ask Susie to call him from class while I finish looking at my email. One of those stealth kids, this boy quiets the usual thunk of sneakers and rustle of clothing and manages to sit in the chair at the round table without my hearing him come in. Tiny bits of blond from a recent hair-color adventure still top the gelled spikes of his brown hair. Fifth-grade cool all over the place, he waits for me to begin. I suspect that these boy rappers were talking big for each other's benefit. Since that kind of speech is still free around here, I decide to use a friendly version of if-you-do-X, then-I'll-have-to-do-Y.

It doesn't take him long to convince me that this is all a misunderstanding, that he and his friends don't plan to sabotage the talent show. Fortunately, we get there without my having to ask what song they are lip-syncing. Since I don't know artists or songs in the category we're dealing with, that information wouldn't help me. I know dirty when I hear it, but on stage the week after next will be too late. I repeat my warning about any funny stuff with the music.

His hair amuses me even more when I see it from the back. When the elementary school kids first started coloring their hair—boys before the girls—I felt too old for this. Even after I gave in to the rainbow of hair, I gritted my teeth when one boy came to kindergarten every day wearing a big gold earring in each lobe. I made it out of there before any of my elementary students showed up tattooed, or pierced in places other than ears.

On the phone, the mother who worried seems satisfied when I tell her that I've spoken to the boy, and that I believe he will not perform off-color material.

My wire basket doesn't contain any of the goldenrod sheets that signal lunchtime behavior troubles, but other notes have stacked up since I last looked. The "good note" Susie mentioned earlier tells me that a 1:15 meeting with the woman from the desegregation committee has turned into a phone conference at 3:30. This delay gives me some relief from the pressure of what must get done in the hours the kids are in school. Other notes tell me that a teacher aide's husband is starting a second round of chemotherapy and that a foster parent in our neighborhood has a new child with some anger issues.

Next, I read the note from my boss' secretary: A school board member wants me to tabulate the number of kids written up for assault this year—by tomorrow. Since I haven't taken time to enter my discipline notes into the database so far this school year, an unruly pile of behavior slips sits near the right-hand edge of my desk. If I haven't put them into the computer by now, there isn't much chance I'll get to it this year. So I'll have to count them by hand. Tomorrow.

Part of the reason discipline reports, including a few for assault, have piled up is that even in the spring of 2001, principals may not yet log on to the district's server from home. When I asked why, they told me that unspecified other members of my household might find their way to confidential information and then misuse it. We were supposed to spend huge hunks of time entering our discipline records or working with the pile of test score data stored on the district's internal website. There was never time to do this during the school day. *But wait,* I would have cried out if anyone had been listening, *I'm willing to work on evenings and weekends, but why should I have to travel to an empty school building to do it?* The year after I retired,

this restriction eased, leaving principals the opportunity
to work around the clock.

A new email arrives. It advises me to take up the missing substitute teacher money with a woman in Payroll I've
never heard of, so I forward my question about the $1,200
to her. Next, I get Mitchell's mom on the phone and spend
three or four minutes telling her about my conversations
with the children and reassuring her that no assault will be
launched on Mitchell today. Once again, I hear those pauses
that suggest she is not saying everything she is thinking.
When we hang up, I worry that I've rushed her off the
phone. I have no idea what I've accomplished by this call.

I look at the next message. It's from a district-level
science coordinator, responding to a question I sent her
the other day.

> Caroline,
>
> I haven't researched the possibility of e-coli
> growing from the sand mixture we use for
> the first grade science lesson, but I will.
>
> Tell the teacher who asked that good hand
> washing prevents students from ingesting
> e-coli. Students shouldn't put their hands in
> their mouths.

Ha! You'd have to tie first graders' hands behind their
backs to keep their little paws out of their mouths.

In the pile of papers on my desk, there's a new phone message from the mother who wants someone to pay for her son's shirt that was damaged in a scuffle at school. I have told her more than once that he was right in the middle of the horseplay that tore the shirt. On top of that, he fiddled with the shirt until the hole got a lot bigger. The torn-shirt boy is Anglo and the alleged perpetrator is Latino. Mom remarked to the teacher that she felt discriminated against because our school was "mostly Mexican." I put this one in a new pile for tomorrow morning.

As I come back from a trip to the restroom, Susie hands me my second note of the day from Patrick's teacher.

Dr. Tompkins,

Patrick pulled his zipper down to show the following students:

Christle

Rodney ("He kicked me and said a bad word")

Jordan

Megan F

CHAPTER 14
SEXUAL HARASSMENT

1993–94, Miller School

ONE MORNING IN THE SPRING of my last year at Miller, I picked up a phone call from the mother of a petite second-grade girl. A boy in this girl's class had been talking to her about the "chi-chis" that she would someday have on her chest, while, thank goodness, he would not. The girl's mom knew what was OK and not OK about body-related talk in her workplace and she didn't see that school should be any different. Why should a girl have to accept treatment that a woman should not? From the beginning, the girl's mom used the phrase *sexual harassment*. I could not disagree with her. This was only a few months after the first time I had used that same phrase about something else that happened at Miller.

The previous November, a fifth-grade boy had asked two friends to hold a girl's arms while he brushed his hand across her breasts, or at least the area of her chest where breasts would soon appear. This happened at the edge of the playground during a recess period while the teacher was tending to some other kids near the building. The girl admitted that she'd let the two boys hold her arms because she thought it was just a game, but she had not told the third boy it was OK to touch her chest. Also thinking it was harmless horseplay, the two arm-holding boys had had no idea what the third boy was about to do, so I let them go with a warning. The boy who'd set up the situation and had done the touching didn't see why I was making such a big deal over a little bit of playing around.

When I called the toucher's parents to tell them I was suspending him from school for two days, his mom put his dad on the phone. In a raised voice, the dad said, "My son is only eleven years old! So maybe he touched her boob by accident. He was just playing around. What's the big deal?" And then he laughed. He went on to say that if she was the kind of girl who fooled around with three boys at a time, then she must have been asking for it, and on and on.

Nan Stein's research on sexualized school bullying had been published—and noted in the newspapers—about a year earlier.[4] Stein applied the term *sexual harassment,* words that had previously been used only for adult misbehavior. She found that student-to-student, usually boy-to-girl, sexualized harassment was showing up regularly in elementary, middle, and high schools. In case the Miller fifth-grader's touch might constitute sexual harassment, I called the school district's civil rights officer to ask him about it.

As we talked, the equity director allowed that sexual harassment might be something that occurred among adults in the workplace, but *not,* he said, between students in a public elementary school. He suggested that my school must be very fringe, or very "unusual," or very *something,* if any boy-to-girl sexualized bothering was going on. Before this, I had known the equity director as someone who cared about discrimination, and not just as someone who managed complaints because it was his job. Had he missed the news reports? This was not long before we heard about a girl in Georgia who won a suit against her school district after administrators didn't stop boys from sex-focused bullying.[5]

Even though I had pulled the two-day suspension out of the air, I stood by it even when the dad protested. Almost immediately, I wished I had made it longer. I phoned a couple of colleagues, but no one could advise me how to handle it. No precedent existed. Apparently, in those days, in my school district, boys would be boys. At the time, it didn't cross my mind that a fifth-grade boy touching a girl's chest was anything more serious than harassment. Years later I realized that the equity officer didn't tell me, or didn't realize, a truth about this: The unwanted, unwelcome touch was assault. I could have called the police.

Now, with the second-grade boy's *"chi-chis"* remarks, I called his mother, but it was his father who called me back later that afternoon. This dad sang the same tune as the fifth grader's father had: "What do you mean, sexual harassment? That's just the way kids talk. What's the matter with girls these days, they can't take anything? He was just having a little fun with her. If you lay a hand on my kid for this, I'll go to the school board."

That second raging dad spurred the next phase of my learning. Sorting out the issue depends partially on the kids' ages. In most states the law doesn't recognize young children as capable of forming criminal intent, but that doesn't mean some second graders, and kids even younger, won't imitate bad deeds they've seen and heard at home or learned from older kids. How sexual were the boy's intentions? The younger the boy, the more difficult it was to evaluate whether he intended to create sexual or body-related discomfort for the girl. Was he using the privilege and power of being male to shame her about her female body? Or was this kid just being a pest, imitating behavior he had witnessed, carrying on a tradition?

In the end, I believed the boy's intentions were gendered without being sexual in the adult sense. Still, I agreed with the girl's mom that sexual harassment was the right label for it. Because he was young, I gave the boy a few days of missed recess and some strict rules about talking to his female classmates. As far as I know, his father did not go to the school board, but his mother's frosty tone and clipped sentences signaled a chill in a relationship that had been cordial up to that time.

Within weeks of the "chi-chis" incident, the mother of a fourth-grade girl called me to complain that a boy had kissed her daughter the day before, and what was I going to do about it? It took me nearly half a day of interviews with what seemed like the entire fourth grade to figure this one out.

First, the boy's friends had asked the girl's friends to find out if she would let him kiss her. At some point, the girl had relayed back an OK. By the time this message made it back to the boy's people from the girl's people, she'd changed her mind, but that never made it back into the grapevine. Both groups of friends gathered to watch the boy plant his lips on the girl's cheek.

Expecting that I should have read the children's minds and flown out to the playground to prevent this relatively innocent one-way show of affection, the girl's mom wouldn't back down in her protest. Hard as it is for a boy to tell when no means no, it is harder still to discern when yes means no, especially when the grapevine is operated by fourth graders.

In the next couple of years, the district added a female staff attorney to its civil rights office, and all of a sudden sexual harassment among kids was on the agenda. As courts around the country were awarding cash settlements to victims when schools failed to stop sexualized bullying, our district sent all the principals to workshops on handling sexual harassment. Even with this support, the situations just got trickier.

Today, 1:04 p.m.

With the end-of-day bell coming up in just under an hour, I need to check on the business of Patrick's zipper while I visit the remaining rooms. I make it only as far as the front lobby when Norma from Mr. McElroy's class slams herself into one of the green chairs and crosses her arms. Norma, it turns out, ordered a second grade boy to kick another second grade boy because of some real or imagined bad look that the victim's sister had given Norma.

The kicker is brand-new to our school and probably felt he had no choice but to do the bidding of this much bigger girl. Instead of bringing him into my office for interrogation and reprimand, I smile and kneel down by the chair where he now sits, his eyes brimming. I tell him I need his help in figuring out what happened. This whole business, including a visit to the health office to see the victim and a stern conversation with an unrepentant Norma, takes fifteen more of the minutes I have left.

As we finish, one of the monitors drops a half-sheet of goldenrod paper into my basket and apologizes for bringing it in late. The referral tells me that a second grader pushed her own sister off the end of the cafeteria bench during lunch. Since she's in the class next to Patrick's, I can see both of them on this trip.

After I see the sister-pusher and make her cry by telling her I'm going to call her mom, I hurry to Patrick's classroom. I find the kids scattered at the teacher's feet listening to a story. Patrick sprawls on the floor with his eyes closed, squeezing out a bogus snore. I ignore the theatrics and whisper the big question into the teacher's ear: "What showed when he pulled down his zipper?"

"I'm pretty sure it was only his underwear. But it got the other kids wound up."

I take the two girls who told on Patrick into the hallway together, violating my own rule of talking to victims and witnesses one by one. I realize quickly that the zipper business happened weeks ago, when someone dared Patrick to do it.

"How come your teacher just found out about it today?" I ask.

"Somebody was teasing Patrick about it and she heard."

I exhale. Patrick's behavior lacks the motive of sexual bullying. It seems to be equal-opportunity grandstanding by a compulsive attention-seeker. I feel grateful for the heads-up from Mrs. Carlson, but a one-time underwear flash by a second grader won't be a big deal in anyone's life story.

1999–2001, Brichta School

In my last two years at Brichta, second-grader Nicholas stalked a classmate in Ḟopes of kissing her; first-grader Pablo touched Vanessa's rear end when he stood below her on the ladder of the playground slide; and second graders Timmy and Coral snuck back into the classroom at recess so they could play "humping," the word they both used matter-of-factly.

The first of these boys, Nicholas, would ambush his classmate Tammy and beg—or even try—to kiss her cheek. Even with Nicholas' parents working with us to stop the behavior, he'd start back up a week or so after each time I told his mom. With the law by then giving Tammy several new rights, I had to find another classroom for Nicholas, one with a different lunch hour and that was far away from his old room. Desperate, I sent Nicholas to his next-year's teacher two months early. In that class, he was too cowed by the older kids to try anything for the rest of the year. This time, his dad was a stepfather who didn't huff and puff at me and who took Nicholas to a counselor.

When Pablo touched Vanessa's rear end on the slide ladder, Vanessa's mom demanded that I suspend Pablo from school. Mom said that she'd been abused when she was little and she wasn't about to let it happen to her daughter. But when I asked Pablo to tell me what had happened, I watched his face carefully, alert for any goofy grin or borderline leer. He seemed genuinely puzzled about all the fuss over a nudge meant only to hurry Vanessa up so he could get to the top and slide down.

After our conversation, I felt satisfied that as a six-year-old, Pablo had no sexualized or even gendered motive. He touched her backside because it was there, not because he was trying to cop a feel or intimidate her. *His* mother, who had two daughters, helped me explain to Pablo why it was a bad idea to touch a girl on a private part of her body if all he wanted was her attention. Pablo seemed to understand and Vanessa got over it sooner than her mother did.

The "humping" incident simmered for quite a while. Timmy was friendly and loved to play with both boys and girls, but he didn't boss other kids around or try to force them to do what he wanted. Coral, no more submissive than Timmy was dominant, had agreed to his suggestions for this fully-clothed "humping" game. They seemed equally curious. Afterward, Coral's very young single mother wouldn't accept that Coral had agreed to play this game with Timmy.

While Timmy's father provided structure and rules in his home, Timmy experienced looser arrangements during weekends with his mother. That home included several teenagers related to the mother's boyfriend. I could only draw clear lines for school behavior and then buffer the blame that flew back and forth between the families, and ultimately, at me.

Today, 1:35 p.m.

In the next fifteen minutes, I watch one kindergarten class start a science lesson and another finish up math games and then take out art supplies. I nearly open Mrs. Sorensen's door before I decide I've been in there enough today, and that I don't want to spark any kind of reaction from Jenifer.

To see my last unvisited class, I go outdoors, where a first grade is swarming over the multi-colored play structure, the latter-day descendant of the jungle gym. As this particular teacher always does, she greets me with a smile and says, "Hi. How are you?" I never know if she respects me or if I am being—have been for all these years—kissed up to. My life on the job works better if I do not question the appearance of sincere-and-earnest, no matter what hard feelings might lurk underneath.

Around a corner, I hear loud laughter coming from inside the small restroom across from the cafeteria. The voices sound too old for the first and second graders from nearby classrooms, so I push open the door. The startled look on the face of the fifth grader standing at the sink tells me that she isn't expecting the principal. I see a pair of feet under the partition that divides the toilet from where she and I stand. I ask why they are using this restroom instead of the one near their class. "Our class is in the computer lab," she says. And of course this is the restroom they are supposed to be using.

"Right, sorry, I didn't mean to pick on you!" I say, smiling, edging away from over-principaling. Once they leave, I notice a wad of bright pink bubble gum caught an inch down in the sink drain, but I stop myself from trying to fish it out with my fingers. I hope I'll remember to tell one of the custodians before it turns into call-a-plumber.

On my way back to the office less than a minute later, I pass the afternoon custodian going in the opposite direction and know there is something I need to ask him to do, but can't remember what. Just then, the end-of-day bell rings and kids burst out of classroom doors and fill the hallway.

CHAPTER 15

REMODELING

1995–98, Brichta School

EVEN WITH THE BUMPINESS of my first year at Brichta, almost all of the teachers stayed on, and I kept up my equal-opportunity approach. At the same time, any progress I made in connecting personally with my new staff was good luck and not strategic. Most of the teachers were cordial and some found me approachable enough to share personal issues that might affect their work.

Each semester, I organized an after-school class for teachers on topics like creating community in classrooms or writers' workshop. Enough teachers signed up each time to make this work, even before the school district offered a stipend for professional learning.

By our third year together, I believe the staff had caught on that I was full of earnest intention even when I got cranky or lacked tact. They had figured out what they could trust me on and what they couldn't. They were willing to sit down as a group to figure things out, to share ideas, and to plan.

Our biggest opportunity to work on something together came when we faced a year-long remodel of the schoolhouse. Before gathering the teachers to figure out the best way to support each other through this, I'd already met with the project manager, the architect, and the contractor about how we'd keep the school running during the construction. The contractor would renovate four classrooms at a time. A bunch of new portables would be trucked in and set up in two rows like facing ranks of barracks, along with a trailer that held boys' and girls' restrooms. An intricate choreography would involve three rotations of classes into and then back out of the added portables between August and May.

Each teacher, except those in the older portables, would have to pack up furniture, books, supplies, and sometimes large personal collections of materials, then unpack everything in one of the temporary buildings, where they'd teach for two to three months. Then they'd reverse the whole process and move back to the freshly painted and newly carpeted classrooms. District workers would help move the packed boxes, but the teachers had to label everything carefully. Some of the teachers would have preferred no remodeling at all. Maybe most of them.

In April, before all this would take place, I gathered the teachers in the library. We talked about how we could manage this as a community and not as a collection of cranky individuals, because cranky is how we all felt about what we faced. I don't remember how many times we met to deal with it, but everyone got to meet the contractor and the construction manager and tell them what we worried about most. We brainstormed ideas for how people could help each other so that no one felt isolated with their move. The teachers in the old portables, the ones who would not have to pack and unpack, stepped forward with generous offers of help.

No one ever expects a construction project to go off without a hitch, and this one didn't, but the on-site construction superintendent never lost sight of the school's primary work, children's learning. He treated me and the staff with respect, communicated consistently and clearly, listened carefully, and kept us to our schedule of planned moves. At various points in the work, staff had a chance to help pick colors for paint, for tile, and for carpet. This was not the best year in any of our lives at school, but I believe it went more easily because we made conscious effort to be in it together.

This gave us important muscle for collaborative work that carried us through a big curriculum change as well. Our school district adopted a new framework for teaching—and then evaluating—student writing. Most of us could see the value of the six-trait rubric scoring system, but we had to learn a lot to make it work. We set up after-school classes for at least two semesters, maybe three. In addition to the small-group work needed to calibrate the new scoring, we spent one semester as a writers' workshop practicing the genre writing we were supposed to teach the kids.

Today, 2:02 p.m.

I hurry outside to help the two bus monitors send the kids home. About 150 children swarm the concrete slab and sidewalks at the south end of the school building, crisscrossing each other's paths as they sort themselves out into two long lines for the neighborhood buses and five shorter lines for the special education buses. The triangular expanse of concrete where the kids line up is bounded by the painted bus curb, the school building, and the staff parking lot. A short chain-link fence separates the slab from the parking area, but only a symbolic yellow stripe cautions children to stand back from the bus bay. The district can't afford to build us a fence that would hold the kids back from the street, so we depend on painted stripes and orange traffic cones to keep our kids safe.

Their bright yellow safety vests help me spot, first, one monitor sorting out the kids waiting for the special education buses, and then a second monitor, trying to solve something for a little kid in the Bus Two line. I'm not sure if I'm a help to the monitors. Sometimes they tell me the kids behave better when I'm on the scene. The raw energy is quite a spectacle when I'm there, so I can't really imagine the alternative. Maybe it counts for something that I see what the monitors face, and that they know I see it.

When I search the crowd for Ricky so we can settle this morning's issue with the bus driver, I see him jumping back and forth across the yellow line, pretending that he is about to fall off the curb. Just as I've spied Ricky, a second-grade boy touches my arm and says that Samuel grabbed his backpack and ran away with it. Banking on Ricky's bus not arriving for another minute or so and on his surviving his latest death defying act, I scan the crowd for Samuel.

Nine years old now, Samuel is an odd boy who whirls around the bus queues, grabbing caps or backpacks. He can only read a few words and add numbers up to six. Counseling, one grade retention, and two rounds of testing have not pointed us in a right direction with Samuel. The small amount of tutoring we offer doesn't seem to help. An average score on one of the ten scales of the IQ test—and below-par scores on the other nine—has ruled out mental retardation. Samuel's mom tells us, "He hardly has any problems at home."

While we watch the other kids, the monitors and I cannot physically hold Samuel. Most days, we sheepdog him the best we can until the bus takes him away or his mother shows up in her car and honks from across the street, gesturing for him to dodge cars and buses to meet up with her. She avoids the regular car pick-up area around the corner, the one that involves lining up and waiting your turn. Today, I spot Samuel crouching behind the kids lined up for Bus One. When I confront him, he won't meet my eyes and twists away from my hand on his arm. I hold out my hand for the backpack and he gives it up without looking at my face. I hand it off to its owner and make my way to Ricky, who has not joined the line-up for his bus.

I use the same shoulder-guiding move I used this morning and march him up the bus steps ahead of the others and plunk him into the seat right behind the driver. I get more tickets—"Bus Conduct Reports"—for Bus One kids than for all the other buses combined. Emotion runs high and plots hatch or develop in the short and crowded trip home. Sharing the same close quarters at the apartment complex and at school, then riding home squashed together, must feel to these kids like being shaken up in a bottle that fizzes over the top.

Even after two years of begging for an onboard monitor to help manage the daily chaos, Myrna receives this assistance only some of the time. I can't imagine what nerves she has left after she drops off her last Brichta kid and starts her middle-school route. Now, as I climb aboard her bus, she shifts slightly in her seat but doesn't say anything. I start, targeting my all-business tone of voice at her and Ricky equally. "I'll suspend him from the bus for a few more days as soon as I get the ticket from this morning." Since this bus is, after all, Myrna's domain, I add, "Is it OK if he sits here behind you now?"

She nods but barely contains a roll of the eyes. As I step off onto the curb, children push past me on their way in. This includes most of the forty who'll get off at the apartments with Ricky. I am surprised when I hear the driver calling out friendly greetings, by name, to lots of kids as they climb aboard. I'm the outsider here.

The line for Bus Two is holding its shape, so I jog over to the little porch outside my office to check on the kids waiting for daycare vans. Just like he does every day, first-grader James sits on the curb and tosses twigs and pebbles up in the air. As always, these unwelcome items land in other kids' clothing and hair. Each time one of us tells James to stop, he looks directly at us and says "I didn't do it," as if our eyes have deceived us.

Once we tried sending a smiley note home for each day James didn't do it, but he remained indifferent to the benefits of this. I don't know if rocks and sticks are part of a compulsion outside of James' control, or just a recurring rotten behavior. Today, I repeat my "knock it off" lecture, and he stops, but I can already picture tomorrow's re-run. James is another kid who's been taken in by relatives who expect their attention to shape him up fast. We hesitate to talk to them about rocks and twigs because they might spank him. However annoying this behavior is, it's not even close to spank-worthy.

With both buses departed now, the two monitors will take care of the five or six kids still waiting for their day-care vans. All at once, it's as if someone has turned off a noisy engine you didn't realize was running. Back inside my office, I refill my plastic water cup from the gallon jug I keep on the bottom shelf by my desk, only the second drink of anything I have had since breakfast. Even with the overhead fluorescents on, my office seems dark after ten minutes in the late winter sunshine.

1995–98, School District

Before public schools existed, teachers often came from monasteries and convents, where they were bound by vows of poverty and chastity. As schools have developed into secular institutions and the profession has developed beyond the bounds of the religious orders, I believe the expectation of earnest personal sacrifice has not altogether disappeared.

By the late twentieth century, teachers and even principals getting married and having babies had become commonplace in public schools, but hovering just off to one side of educators' public faces were divorces, cancer, depression, mental illness, alcohol and drug abuse. Once I became a principal, it didn't take me long to discover that it was part of my job to help maintain the illusion of the chaste and bland teacher, someone who didn't experience the same life challenges as the rest of their community.

During my first year at Miller, an unmarried teacher came to my office one day and said, "I'm pregnant. On purpose. I'm due in April. I'm not getting married." She went on to tell me that the baby's father wouldn't be involved and that her parents fully supported her decision and would come to town to help her when the baby arrived. She planned to return to her job the next year.

When this happened in the 1980s, public schools were still sorting out the collision between individual employee rights and traditional social values. This woman gave birth to her son less than twenty years after Tucson began allowing teachers to stay in their classrooms once the pregnancy was obvious, and it was assumed that these teachers were married. I left it up to her to decide what she would tell her third graders and their parents. More than twenty-five years later, neither the teacher nor I remembers how she notified them, but not a one of them said anything to me about it.

During my last year at Miller, another unmarried teacher became pregnant by accident, and the kids and their parents threw a baby shower for her near the end of the year. Other than expressing concern about how this unexpected turn of events would affect a young teacher they cared about, no one said a word to me on this occasion either.

Teachers have formed and joined unions to push back against explicit and implicit pressure to sacrifice themselves. Organizing has helped them obtain fairer salaries, better working conditions, reasonable limits on work hours, clear contractual language, and representation in disputes with administration. When I had to handle the staff reduction during my first year at Miller, I memorized large chunks of the union contract so that I'd be sure to follow the rules. Before long, I knew the document well and carefully followed each year's revisions. Teachers at both Miller and Brichta often asked me to interpret or explain language in the contract, trusting that I knew these details as well as their union representative.

Not long after I became a principal, the wave of education reform I'd been riding began to give way to something else that also called itself "reform," but was very different. I was still caught up in the version of reform that explored and embraced shared decision-making, diverse teaching strategies, inquiry-based learning, and varied forms of assessment. I didn't catch on quickly that my reform had been overtaken, even steamrolled, by a top-down version of control that emphasized uniformity and conformity, limited categories of "results" and "outcomes," tests of questionable value, and punishments for not measuring up.

For most of my time at Brichta, we still had the tall three-piece-suit superintendent and the deputy superintendent who believed we could engineer human learning. If you look at motivation as being "carrot" or "stick," we had definitely entered "stick" territory. Not only were we pushed to set higher achievement test score goals for our schools, we were often handed goals and targets that were based on pure fantasy. At meetings, we were nagged and threatened about student achievement, while actual learning was rarely mentioned. The superintendent once invited principals to a reception and then walked up to individuals and made critical comments to them about their schools' test scores. I managed to miss this event, but heard talk about it for many months.

During this same time, the school board hired an in-house attorney who treated middle management—the principals and assistant principals—as both enemies and slaves of the administrators above us. Principals had contracts that specified leave and vacation, but the attorney informed us that there was no such thing as off-duty. We were to show up or be available for phone calls at any time of any day throughout the calendar year. If a summer meeting was set up for a time we were off-contract and had travel plans, we were expected to cancel the trip. These orders remained unwritten, but word-of-mouth was enough to keep us in line. I'd been working in the school district for nearly twenty years, and this was the first time we'd not been considered part of the team.

Seven or eight principals on our side of town met for breakfast once a month. Officially, we were supposed to talk about helping our kids make the move from elementary to middle school, a leap more like landing on another planet than like moving from one building to another. The elementary principals had seen too many vulnerable kids lose their way in middle school. We lacked the clout to dictate a child-welcoming environment in sixth, seventh, and eighth grades, so we looked for ways to cushion the shock.

For the first couple of years, we spent most of our time together talking about the kids' transition from elementary to middle school. We discussed curriculum, made plans for the annual fifth grade visit, and brainstormed ways to blunt some of the fear that the younger kids felt when they moved up. As we reached the second half of the 1990s, our talk about the move to middle school seemed to finish earlier in our meetings, and we spent more time talking about violent kids, test score pressures, tightened budgets, and the flood of new directives from central office.

During the fourth or fifth year of these gatherings, I arrived early to one of the meetings and started chatting with a new colleague. Out of nowhere, she began talking fast about how she and sixty percent of her faculty took anti-depressants. She said that the whole bunch of them talked with each other about their prescriptions, comparing Prozac with Celexa, discussing dosages, and so on. I wondered if sixty percent of my faculty used medication to fight depression. I would have guessed about a third, but didn't feel it was something I could ask.

One day, the insurance department cut off a teacher's health coverage because someone in human resources misplaced a form. Later that morning, after a fast drive downtown, I sat through the guilty party's entire lunch hour waiting for her to return. When I showed no signs of leaving, she surprised herself by locating the misplaced form in the top drawer of her filing cabinet. I did it again when the payroll office "didn't have time" to enter a new employee into their database by the end of the second pay period of the year. I might not be able to fix every kid, avert natural disasters, or guarantee everyone's safety in an open-door campus, but once in a while I could apply pressure until I got a result.

Those moments of drama should not suggest that all the secretaries and administrative assistants who worked in the many centralized departments were lazy, stupid, or incompetent. Only a very few of them were. Most were smart, committed, and hardworking women who gave me wonderful help in both routine and out-of-the-ordinary situations. They themselves ridiculed the convoluted district regulations, the multiple layers and signatures required to accomplish routine tasks, and the new computer systems that could never quite handle complex work.

Today, 2:14 p.m.

After seeing the kids off on their buses and vans, I arrive a little late to our Child Study meeting. The counselor arrives at the same time, and everyone crowds a little closer together to make room for the two of us around the absurdly small table. It offers work space to four children, and here we sit, eight adults, nowhere to put our knees. In this weekly team meeting, the learning disabilities specialist, the counselor, a speech therapist, a school psychologist, a social worker, and several teachers, along with me, sit together to talk about kids who puzzle us. At each meeting, one teacher tells the rest of the team about two children whose needs seem to outstrip her resources.

We are talking about Jakob first, and on the table I spy a paper with JaKod penciled at the top. I ask, "How old was his mother when Jakob was born?"

"Seventeen," says our once-a-week social worker, who met with Jakob's mother a few days ago to ask about his life so far.

Jakob's mom, now in her mid-twenties, has not pushed us to test him. If she had, we might have bumped him closer to the front of the line for Child Study. Today, Jakob's teacher tells us that Jakob's mom had a new baby in January and that Jakob doesn't say much about his new brother. Sometimes he talks about his stepdad but doesn't seem to be getting much attention from his mom. One of us notices that Jakob has missed twenty school days in his first six months with us, including ten Mondays between September and January. The average child misses eight to ten days of school each year for all of the usual reasons, colds, flu, medical appointments, and short family trips.

I recall that Jakob's mother works at a hair salon that closes on Mondays. His teacher says, "Oooh. Sorry I didn't catch that Monday business. No wonder he never knows what we're supposed to be doing. That's when I introduce the centers and give the spelling words."

We spend the next ten minutes asking ourselves whether Jakob's learning problems come from missing so much school or from a learning disability, or both. We decide to give Mom a clear condition: If she gets him to school every day, or nearly, for the rest of the year, we'll offer him the testing in the fall. We also agree to tell her that if this attendance pattern continues, Jakob will almost certainly not do well enough to pass to the next grade.

CHAPTER 16
TUAN

1998, Brichta School
HALFWAY THROUGH MY fifth year at Brichta, a cafeteria monitor tracked me down four days in a row to tell me that a boy named Tuan was climbing up onto a cafeteria table, then screaming and kicking. She described how he tried to push the other kids' trays and lunch boxes off the table and wouldn't do anything she told him to. "He kicks me. He gets on top of the table and takes off his shoes and throws them on the floor. Then he takes off his shirt," she told me. Next, Tuan climbed down from the table and ran behind the stage curtains and screamed some more.

Partway through the school year, Tuan's family had moved from a small agricultural community in another part of Arizona, where his school had had only about one hundred students altogether. Tuan's mother told us that he had been in a very small class, one with only five kids and three teachers. We took this to mean one teacher and two teacher aides, or five kids and three adults. Our class had twelve kids, one teacher, and one aide who happened to be out on a long-term sick leave. We could only get a substitute for the aide a couple of days each week.

Tuan's records were difficult to sort out, possibly because very small school districts often handle these things in a more personal than systematic way. In those days, our school district and many others wanted to avoid giving certain labels to special needs kids from ethnic minority groups. Tuan's parents were from Southeast Asia, and nine-year-old Tuan had been born eight years after his next-oldest sibling. Tuan's Individualized Educational Program, or IEP, said he was supposed to get lunch in the cafeteria with the other third and fourth graders, who would help him learn good social behavior. This one provision alone involved several layers of bad assumptions for our larger school and its busy cafeteria.

By the middle of the first week, Tuan's constant outbursts in class had exhausted his teacher, who was both capable and resourceful. Each day, she updated me on how things had gone, what she would try tomorrow. That year, Tuan's teacher had most of the same kids

who'd be in Ms. Langer's class my last year at Brichta.
When a new child arrived to be in the class, the others
had to test every limit all over again. The herbs Tuan's
mother gave him didn't seem to help, and Tuan's father
said as long as we would not take a strap to Tuan the
way he did, we would never get anywhere with him.

Teachers were always supposed to get a half hour
for lunch with no kids to watch. Early in our conversations about Tuan, his teacher said she needed this
time, that she didn't want to give it up to stay in the
room with Tuan. I agreed with her: She was entitled
to it, and *every* teacher needs a kid-free lunch break.
I could not take Tuan every day because I had to be
on deck for everything else, including filling in for the
missing cafeteria worker when food services couldn't
send a substitute.

I suggested that the *aide-du-jour*, when we had one,
should go with Tuan first to the cafeteria and then to
the playground, where she'd stay close to him, then
eat her own lunch after everyone else was back in the
classroom. The teacher agreed to this, knowing that
it would only help on the couple of days a week when
we could get the substitute assistant.

Tuan's daily outbursts had gone on for just over a
week when a mother I especially liked phoned to set
a time to meet with me. Her daughter had told her
a troubling story, and she wanted to discuss it with
me in person.

"It's about that boy, the one who gets on the table and screams," the mother started. She went on to tell me how her daughter had brought her lunch home untouched the last three days. She'd told her mom that she'd tried to eat, but that boy screaming and taking his clothes off had upset her stomach. "I'm sorry to bother you with this, but I think my daughter and the other kids are entitled to eat in peace." She sat back in her chair and gave me a slight smile, waiting for me to offer a solution.

Before this, I had always been happy to see this nice mom. Now, I could do nothing to solve her problem without making a problem for someone else. And everyone's problems were my problems.

I said, "You're right. This has been a terrible situation. The way the Special Ed rules work, Tuan has the right to eat in the cafeteria. I haven't found a way . . ." and suddenly I started sobbing and couldn't stop. All I could say was, "I'm sorry, this has been really hard for me. I'm sorry. I don't know why I'm crying. I'm sorry. I'll see if I can figure something out. I'm really sorry." My visitor stayed for a few more minutes, just to make sure I was going to be OK. Once she'd left, Susie came in to check on me.

Today, 2:37 p.m.

Our child study meeting has moved on from Jakob and we're talking about Patrick. He has exasperated and amused us in the nearly two years we've known him. Patrick talks like a short adult who has seen and done everything. His seven-year-old swagger suggests that he is about to whip out a deck of cards and ask you to pick one.

His teacher tells us that Patrick's white and apparently middle-class parents, with whom he lives as their only child, never answer notes home or return calls. I remember seeing them only once in the time Patrick has been here. In *my* white middle-class gut I don't get how some parents can hold themselves at such a distance from their children's schooling. His teacher likes Patrick, but his constant bids for attention wear her down.

"Once he hooks me into telling him to sit back down, he launches into a big explanation of what he's doing. These are always weird, like, when he's at the sink without permission, 'My uncle told me to wash my hands before I crack open peanuts.'" We laugh together even though this is the wrong kind of funny. The team knows how this eats minutes from Mrs. Carlson's teaching or from her scarce planning time. The other kids seem to respond to Patrick's lone-wolf nature by not inviting him to play with them.

His teacher tells us about a reading test she gave Patrick. He fumbled about half the words, but just kept on going. He more-or-less summarized a paragraph, but had funny ideas about the details. His handwriting is immature, but not messy and all over the page like Jakob's. Patrick uses an extravagant vocabulary for his age, saying "drowsy" and "excellent" and "according to my father." He does OK in math.

We give Mrs. Carlson a few suggestions for helping him put together the pieces of what he reads, and then we turn to the behavior. Our short-term goal is that Patrick behave better in class so there are fewer disruptions to teaching and learning. Because he's basically a good-natured kid, and not aggressive, we want to come up with a plan that relies entirely on positive feedback and modest rewards. I have an idea, but I hold back a minute from saying it so others have a chance to speak.

When no one else says anything, I ask, "How about giving Patrick some time to follow Jason around if he reduces his goofy behavior in class?" Having a child "help" the custodian is one of our limited options in a building that lacks enough Somebodies to go around. Jason is our young afternoon custodian, the one we are trying to nudge off to college. Heads nod, shoulders shrug. It will be my job to get permission from Patrick's mom to do this.

In the next three or four minutes, we write up our plan. For each half day Patrick makes a good effort in the classroom, he will earn a few minutes working alongside Jason. We have made plans like this for other kids with modest success. Does the team really go along or have I just principaled the room so rigidly that they're afraid to disagree?

At 3:10, we unfold ourselves from our places around the low table. In the hallway, I ask the counselor if Ricky told her that his stepmom has left the family. The counselor's mouth opens a bit and her eyebrows rise while she says, "No." But we don't have time to talk about it now.

1995–98, The Wellness Committee

With two of my colleagues from the board of our administrators' association, I started a Wellness Committee. Hoping to find out what troubled our members, we sent out a detailed questionnaire about satisfaction and frustration on the job. We thought we'd use the results to open the eyes of our bosses, who might then *do* something to help. Looking back, this seems naïve in the extreme.

Some of the administrative layers between *us*, the principals, and *them*, the superintendent and the deputy, included competent and caring people. Unlike superintendents and some other top leadership who came from distant cities and left us for other distant cities, most of our assistant superintendents at that time had come up through the system and had a connection with the community. Each assistant supervised and supported thirty or more principals. Based on the consideration they'd shown so far, I thought they'd pay attention to our survey results.

We sent the wellness survey out to principals and assistant principals, elementary to high school, and even to some mid-level central office administrators. We got back about half of the forms we'd sent out, perhaps

125 in all. I sat down with the two other members of the committee over several weeks to tally and make sense of the responses. Our results told us that more than half of our colleagues were very unhappy at work.

Some of our colleagues admitted to barely holding on. Depression was only one of the issues. Stomach troubles, sleeplessness, high blood pressure, and marital discord all made the list. As a group, the principals felt that unreasonable time demands, mixed messages, lack of support from supervisors, and the galloping growth of the job were seriously harming our effectiveness, our self-confidence, and our family lives.

Every principal I knew did her very best to face the staff and the public as if none of the above affected the school's normal rhythms or our personal equanimity. My job sometimes felt like myth maintenance, keeping alive the notion that the only change since the 1950s was the invention of computers.

Meanwhile, I could see that the assistant superintendents, too high in the pecking order to be included in our survey, were treading water with one arm and using the other to keep the principals afloat along with them. I'd gotten to know and like these assistant superintendents over the years, and I believed that most of them genuinely cared about the principals. I worried about how much it cost them to protect us. I decided that our survey findings would only aggravate their burden. Like a child who wants to protect a parent from bad news, I packed up our returned questionnaires and our tables of results without even writing a summary.

Today, 3:14 p.m.
Back in the office after Child Study, I delete two junk email messages and find that a clerk in Payroll has already replied to the question I sent about the missing $1,200. The clerk explains that a software glitch is charging another school's substitute teacher expense to our budget. "Sorry," she writes. "Brichta comes before the middle school in the alphabet, so since the teacher works at both schools, the system takes the money from the school first in the alphabet." She suggests that I ask the secretary at the other school to fill out a paper form every two weeks to adjust the charge away from us and to her school's budget. Even though we are first in the alphabet, we are not allowed to do this paperwork for some reason that is never explained.

Before I talk to the desegregation committee member at 3:30, I need to find a folder in today's—or this week's—pile and check the notes I penciled in the margins of a report I sent in recently, part of the federal court's monitoring of our compliance with the order.

In the later 1950s, some Anglo families built homes on a hillside west of the Rio Santa Cruz and north of downtown. This new neighborhood sat about a mile from two of the riverbank schools that served darker-skinned and poorer children. The Anglo families soon balked at sending their kids to the schools at the bottom of the hill, the ones that had served Mexican-heritage families up to that point, and petitioned the district's governing board for a new school.

Responding to the Anglo families' request, the board agreed to build a new school halfway up the hill. In naming the new school, the board honored Tucson's first public school teacher, Augustus Brichta. Brichta, a former saloon-keeper, taught his students in Spanish for a few months in the 1860s until the $500 allocated for schooling ran out. His namesake school opened its six rooms in 1960.

Eighteen years later, a federal court ruled that Brichta had been built with "segregative intent." In 1978, the court declared that kids would be bused out of their neighbor-hoods in a shuffle among Brichta and two of the downhill schools.

1999, Brichta School

A couple of hours after I'd cried in my meeting with the upset mother, our daytime custodian, Gabriel, stood in my doorway holding Tuan in his arms. Tuan clung to Gabriel's neck, hiding his face. "I'm afraid he'll hurt himself," Gabriel said.

I invited Tuan to sit down at the round table, but he just held on and buried his face in Gabriel's shirt. Gabriel spoke to Tuan quietly and got him to let go enough that he could be lowered on to one of my blue chairs. As he left, Gabriel said, "Bye, Tuan." To me he said, "I'll have one of the other kids bring his lunch over."

Tuan looked at Gabriel but said nothing. This was Tuan's second or third trip to my office. Like Jenifer would do two years later, he had spent one of these visits huddled under the table. But now he stayed in the chair and I didn't start in on him about the behavior. Instead, I made him an offer: "Would you like to color while you wait for your lunch?"

I gave him some crayons and paper. By the time Gabriel returned with Tuan's lunch, Tuan had used the crayons to draw three yellow stick figures and two blue ones. All five drawings had round heads, smaller circles for eyes and noses, and straight lines where the mouths would be. Legs descended directly from the heads. Stick arms pointed stiffly out to each side from the upper part of the stick legs, and anywhere from four to six lines protruded from the circles at the ends of the stick arms. Tuan was nine, but these were the drawings of a four-year-old.

I did some checking and found that Tuan had been regarded as "untestable" when he'd first arrived in our school district. This meant that an approved test had *not* shown him, *for certain*, to function at the low level we suspected. Under the rules of "least restrictive environment," the school district wanted to put him in a class with low-average kids to see how he would do. If that didn't work, they'd look for a class considered "more restrictive," smaller, with more adults, like the one he'd attended in the smaller town he'd come from. But, first, we'd try to save the taxpayers some money by putting him in the larger class with fewer adults.

Next, our school psychologist, not the one who'd originally sent Tuan to Brichta, looked at Tuan's crayoned self-portraits and agreed that he needed to be re-evaluated. That would require several weeks at minimum, and we had to get through this time as best we could. Tuan's teacher and I decided to break the law, to violate his IEP. No matter what his paperwork said, we would keep Tuan in a quiet place for lunch.

Some days my frustration got the better of me and I called people downtown who were supposed to be in charge. They had no more idea than I did how to work with the kids I call "physically impossible," kids we were not to restrain, lift, or carry if all they were doing was creating chaos. Technically, these children had to be a danger to self or others before physical force could be applied, and then who was supposed to apply it? Whose job description included this? I was sent to special training in deflecting or restraining children's dangerous moves, but the school district got more liability cover from this than I got useful skills.

As we waited for the assigned school psychologist to complete Tuan's re-evaluation, his teacher shouldered the burden of protecting him from too much stimulation while she shielded the other kids against his frantic responses. The rest of us would be dealing with someone or something else and would forget to go and relieve her for lunch. Every once in a while we got a good enough substitute aide and the teacher could leave Tuan for fifteen minutes and eat a quick sandwich in the lounge. Even with this, Tuan broke down in class two or three times each day.

The other kids in his class gradually learned to leave Tuan alone, except for a girl who crowded him whenever she could just to watch him spin out. The new evaluation showed, finally, that Tuan qualified for a smaller class a couple of miles away. This one offered more help for his combination of very low ability and emotional issues.

PART 3
SEEKING SAFETY

During a long, talky evening back in 1962, my high school friend Pat posed this question: "If you lie on your back and put a sheet of paper on your face, and just lie there for a really long time, will the paper eventually crush you?" I told her that was ridiculous.

CHAPTER 17

THREAD OF PRIVILEGE

Today, 3:20 p.m.

WHILE I'M SCRAMBLING TO review the desegregation report before the phone call in ten minutes, Ms. Langer, the special needs teacher, stops by my office. She bears the good news that the boy who screeched and spread the papers across the floor when I came to her room this morning "mostly" settled down after I left. Experience tells me that she wants to know that I don't blame her for what he did, and I volunteer that reassurance and add a compliment about how well one of her other kids seems to be doing.

Susie stops in to tell me about today's "leftover" child. Four days out of five, we have at least one child remaining after all the other kids are gone. Today, Benjy, a first-grader, didn't board his bus because he thought someone was picking him up, but he couldn't quite remember who. I step out the door to take a look, to make sure I know which Benjy is still with us. Dark haired, slumped in one of the reception chairs, he looks as if he's been sleeping and just woke up.

Susie has tracked down Benjy's dad, who apologized and said he'd had to take a family member to the hospital. But he can't get to school until around 4:15. Because federal work rules do not allow me to keep either of my office ladies past 4:00 to wait with Benjy, I'll be the particular Somebody who'll keep an eye on him until his father gets here.

Since I have a few minutes left before the phone call, I tell Susie about Payroll's advice for fixing the substitute budget. I ask if she, Susie, has some ideas for approaching the secretary at the middle school about the monthly paperwork this will require. I tell her we can talk about the playground monitors after my phone call.

The Past

I didn't all at once understand the thread of privilege that still wound through Brichta when I arrived in 1994, a thread that had all but disappeared by the time I left. When I first got there, the neighborhood children no longer rode buses to the surrounding schools, but the ongoing court order still required special attention to our multicultural status.

In the state's classification system, the majority of our students were coded "Hispanic," but only a few were native Spanish speakers. While some lived in the two apartment complexes at the east end of our boundaries, others lived in the foothills to the west of us in good-sized homes on three acres, some with horse corrals. Most of our families lived in the neighborhoods that lay in the big middle, on streets with names like Wagon Wheel that were lined with three-bedroom houses on a quarter-acre.

During my third year at Brichta, a developer built hundreds of apartments across the ravine to the south of us, all of them eligible for a Section 8 rental subsidy. These apartment clusters seemed to attract people who had left extended family behind, emotionally as well as geographically, in California, North Carolina, Mexico, or just on the other side of town.

In my time there, Brichta accommodated a rainbow of heritages, languages, and economic conditions. The once middle-class community was absorbing a complex mix of drug-endangered children and economically fragile families. In the ranch-style homes around Brichta, stable grandparents raised grandchildren while neighborhood parents took on foster children. At least one family started a group home for children who were wards of the state. These trends seemed to accelerate during my seven years.

I began to realize that not all the horse-property families were sending their kids to Brichta. One parent, a surgeon, told me that he "always" sent his children to private school after third grade. A journalism professor I knew from when she'd covered the school district for a local newspaper visited me at Brichta one day. Following a friendly walk around the building, she told me that even though she and her husband had bought a home in the Brichta area, she was looking for a magnet school nearer to her work. In my last couple of years, some families took their kids out and told us they were trying one of Arizona's new charter schools.

After I retired, I looked up U.S. Census figures for the year 2000. I saw that the neighborhoods surrounding Brichta ranged from thirty-five to forty-five percent Latino. When I retired in 2001, Brichta's student body was sixty percent Latino. I don't know if anyone at central office ever caught on that Brichta's numbers reversed the census figures.

When I started at Brichta, my new boss was an assistant superintendent who'd only recently taken over that part of the district. She never did invite me in to discuss the desegregation program before she moved on and someone else took her place.

Today, 3:31 p.m.

The extra money the state sends us because of the court order keeps our classes down to 22 and 23 kids and lets us purchase extra multicultural learning materials. Most importantly, it also pays for a fulltime librarian and counselor and a half-time English teacher for kids who speak another language at home. Any principal would want these extras, which are basic in states that spend more than Arizona on their public schools.

I like the woman who serves on the citizens' committee that watches over the schools that operate under court scrutiny. While I know my job is to represent the district, our conversations are not difficult. Even so, I still wish that someone in central office had taken time with me to discuss our program's purpose as Brichta has diversified far beyond its origins as the school with segregative intent.

I get her on the phone a minute or two after 3:30, and she starts right in with questions. She wants to know which cultural performances we have been able to send kids to, which concerts of dance or music our kids attended at the university or the community college. After a few more routine questions, she asks why the teachers do not use more Spanish in the bilingual classes we offer in grades kindergarten through third.

She and I have talked before about middle-class Latino parents who speak English at home and want their children to learn Spanish in school, often to honor heritage or to understand grandparents. Others want the bilingual class so that they, the parents, can speak Spanish with the teacher. A small group of our Latino parents want nothing to do with bilingual education, and their children learn in English with support from the part-time ESL teacher.

Months ago, in a less formal discussion, the desegregation representative and I found that we understood these preferences and arrangements and didn't have to review them every time we spoke. Even so, in this official conversation, I hesitate to say that the few good Spanish speakers in each class have never added up to critical mass, leaving us challenged to immerse the English speakers in this second language for even half an hour each day. I stay careful and emphasize that a few children, maybe four or five in each class, speak mainly Spanish and are learning English while getting basic skills support in their mother tongue. I don't say how much more robust, how genuinely dual-language, I wish these programs were.

As we continue, I remember that our K–3 bilingual program is not covered by the court order, and that her interest is personal. So I risk a personal view as well, saying not for the first time, "I wish all the kids here, all the kids in Tucson, could learn Spanish in school." After about fifteen minutes, she runs out of questions and I don't offer answers to the ones she hasn't asked. I hang up the phone and tell Susie I have a minute for the playground monitor issue.

1986, Miller School

During my first week as a brand-new principal at Miller Elementary, maybe ten days before the kids would show up for classes, my secretary told me I had a call from a woman whose name I did not recognize. In a friendly voice, the woman on the phone welcomed me to my new job, and then mentioned that not only did her son go to Miller, but she worked at school as a monitor and teaching assistant. Monitor? Before I could get a grip on *monitor*, she said that she wished to stop monitoring and just work her teacher aide hours.

Still not getting what she was talking about, I said "Sure. No problem." After all, I was brand new.

Before fifteen minutes passed, a second woman called. She said she'd heard that my earlier caller had resigned from being the cafeteria monitor. Since she, my second caller, had been monitoring next-longest, could she inherit the indoor monitoring job? This meant supervising the cafeteria at lunchtime rather than patrolling the sunny and often hot schoolyard.

I understood what it meant to be more senior or less senior in a job, so I had a vague idea what she meant. Even so, I didn't imagine yet how the education enterprise can rest on things like having enough monitors in the right places. Now I had four brand new things to juggle: monitors, teacher aides, seniority, and indoors vs. outdoors. That first day, annoyance flashed. I had not become a principal for this. With twenty minutes more experience than I'd had in the first call, I said to my second caller, "I'll have to get back to you on that."

When we located the list of last year's monitors, I called the two who hadn't phoned us yet to find out who'd be showing up on the first day of school. Of the four monitors set to come back, I had just let one escape while another was hanging by a thread. By the end of the day, I'd found that monitors only got paid minimum wage, while teacher aides got closer to a third more. I had no idea where or how a principal found monitors. It turned out that you kept your monitors by offering them work that combined the playground supervision with classroom aide time so they didn't earn so very little. This strategy insured a steady stream of monitors, and I had just tampered with a fine-tuned system by letting my cafeteria monitor out of the deal.

Today, 3:46 p.m.

When Susie and I sit down at my round table, I notice a smudge of cheese next to the spot where Jenifer ate. I feel a poke of embarrassment for not noticing this when Rosie's grandfather sat there four hours ago. I swipe at the spot with a tissue. Susie says, "The other monitors are fed up with Sandy being late all the time."

In any school, when a playground or cafeteria monitor starts showing up late, or just stands in the shade instead of circulating, or gets too tight with one group of kids, or shields her own child from the rules, the others start grumbling. Over the years at both of my schools, the best monitors got better jobs while the indifferent ones drifted away. I fired a few who cursed in front of the kids or missed too much work. One quit after I cautioned her about wearing tight and low-cut clothing.

Susie and I decide to invite the four monitors to a half-hour meeting after lunch on Friday. I'll ask them to tell me how things are going. Then, we'll talk about the cafeteria line turmoil and they will tell me how hard it is to keep order when one has to work solo until the other one arrives. I'll declare just how much *everyone* needs to be on time so you don't let your colleagues down. They'll have a chance to complain about a bunch of things, including the kids' behavior. I'll talk about how overworked and underpaid they are. The pizza for the Friday meeting will cost me $20 of my own money, and it will be worth it.

CHAPTER 18
A NEW NORMAL

1999, Brichta School

SHORTLY AFTER TUAN LEFT BRICHTA for his new class, a family moved to our neighborhood and enrolled their daughter Holly in fourth grade. Holly's parents were middle class, educated, and employed. They told us that Holly had ADHD, that they gave her a pill for it at home each morning. In her previous school, Holly had already qualified for the once-a-week gifted class, and we found out quickly that she could read and compose stories far above her grade level.

We also noticed that instead of working on her math or other assignments, Holly played endlessly with the little toys that came with fast-food kids' meals. She stayed absorbed in these toys and cards for months, even after one sales campaign had given way to the next. Holly loved My Little Pony and collected dozens of related trinkets. She snuck these into her backpack or pockets and then to the top of her school desk. Her detailed pencil drawings based on the obsession *du jour* soon filled one notebook and spilled over into another.

Despite her parents' best efforts to check Holly's backpack for contraband every morning, she still managed to smuggle in a new item nearly every day. Her teacher gave up strict enforcement of the blockade because Holly could bring the entire classroom to a halt if she was told to put the toy away.

Standardized testing week arrived, and we wanted the whole class to do as well as they possibly could. Furthermore, we hoped that Holly would score very high in reading comprehension and boost her class' average, something we knew she could do when she was calm and focused. We decided to go ahead and risk testing Holly along with her class. The reading passages and questions were straightforward and well within her capability. I was in my office when the teacher told her kids to pick up their pencils and open their test booklets.

Holly's teacher would tell me later that she read the directions, worked the examples with the class, set a timer for 40 minutes, and told the students to begin. Within five minutes, Holly started tapping a plastic pony against her desk. The teacher first tried to get the toy away without any commotion, but Holly started rocking and chanting, "No. No. No."

Not even knowing if it was legal in the world of standardized tests, the teacher told the class to stop and close their test booklets. Maybe there was a way they could start again later, have 35 minutes to go on and finish. The teacher didn't see how that could be worse than Holly's outburst messing up the other kids' concentration. Next, the teacher called the office and asked me to come to the room. I found Holly gripping the sides of her desk with both hands. I asked her to come with me and she just swung her head side to side, punctuating the movement with more "No. No. No." I told the teacher to take the other kids outside for a break.

Once I was alone with Holly, she stayed lost in her chant and didn't notice right away that the others had gone. Even without knowing yet what had happened, I wanted to get her out of there, to see if we could circle back to the calm and quiet we needed for testing the rest of the class. Susie, the office manager, answered my intercom call right away and said she would call for one of Holly's parents to come. Then she'd find some-one to help me out. Meanwhile, I watched Holly. The couple of times she seemed to relax a little, I invited her to leave with me, but she only grasped the desk harder. In a stroke of luck, the once-a-week teacher of the gifted was in the building that day to help with testing. Susie figured this out and sent her to me at the ten-minute mark of the impasse.

The visiting teacher and I managed to get Holly partway to the office without physically hauling her there, but then we lost her to a corner. She huddled there, now in tears, until her father arrived. He coaxed Holly into the car and drove away. The next day, Holly was back, but her teacher and I decided together that we could not risk the other kids' scores, so I gave Holly the rest of the tests in my office.

Like any principal in the district who had exhausted her own bag of tricks, I could fill out a form asking for help with a troubled child. Days or weeks later, a specialist would arrive, all positive intention, bringing a standardized formula and some little toys and trinkets that the teacher or I were supposed to present to the child as behavior improved.

This method rested on the assumption that all children could, either through Pavlovian reflex or logic, *choose* their behavior. The chance of a reward, usually a cheap toy, was supposed to trigger this implicit or explicit choosing mechanism. This brand of positive reinforcement only went a short distance with a child who was bipolar or obsessive-compulsive, or one who heard voices.

Holly's teachers, the counselor, the visiting behavior specialists, and I charted her ups and downs, letting her earn rewards or lose privileges. Nothing we offered motivated her out of her biochemical or neurological straitjacket. Holly probably weighed seventy pounds on the day near the end of fourth grade when her dad had to carry her, screaming and flailing, to the car. That trip resulted in Holly's next psychiatric evaluation. A new diagnosis of obsessive-compulsive disorder brought a change in medications that seemed to help, at least some of the time.

Even with new medication, Holly's fixations on certain toys, games, drawings, words and phrases increased. Not even the most patient teacher—and I was grateful she had one both years—could dislodge her from her obsession of the moment without an eruption or a mute withdrawal. She pulled into herself even more and suspected others of being against her. Too often, the entire class remained hostage to a location they needed to leave, held back from wherever they were to arrive next. Even after Holly turned ten at the end of her first year at Brichta, she never showed any embarrassment or self-awareness, just occasional puzzlement when a person acted distant or wary after they'd had a bad time with her.

By the end of Holly's second year with us, her parents were hopeless and defensive and often hostile toward whichever of us had called them to come to school. When I contacted district administrators about ill children who would not or could not follow rules and directions or respond to authority, they looked right through me and changed the subject.

Today, 4:00 p.m.

While Susie and Mary gather up their belongings and head out, I bring Benjy into my office. He can draw while I write up the two teacher evaluations for tomorrow. In defiance of local fire codes, I stuff a rubber wedge under my office door to keep it open. This way, we can hear Benjy's dad if he knocks on the now-locked outer door. It should take me about forty minutes to finish the two evaluations. The easy one, the one for Mr. McElroy, needs only about ten of those minutes, but Ms. Burnett's write-up will take longer.

The steps of the annual evaluation are specified in the teacher contract. The usual pace of drop-in-for-a-minute, exchange a few words passing in the hallway, leave a note, answer a note, shifts to something altogether more awkward and stilted, something over-prescribed and not completely authentic. I scheduled visits with both Mr. McElroy and Ms. Burnett, the teachers whose evaluation forms I'll complete today. I reviewed their lesson plans and slipped into their rooms for at least a half hour each.

Ms. Burnett is in her second year of teaching, and I don't know if she's going to make it. I scan my handwritten observation notes. Without the formal observations, those half hours when a teacher tries to do her very best, I might not have realized the extent of the disarray in Ms. Burnett's room. One morning last week, I found most of the flat-topped desks facing away from the room's front chalkboard, left that way from an art activity the week before. I watched the students twist in their chairs and crane their necks to see what Ms. Burnett was printing in small letters on the board.

On that same visit, I saw Ms. Burnett use a too-easy article on farm animals to teach reading to a group of kids whose squirming I could not hold against them. Kids who were not in that reading group either finished or gave up on seatwork assignments before the end of the allotted 25 minutes. Kids need plenty of support in making good use of their time and in functioning independently when not under the direct gaze of the teacher. Had Ms. Burnett established no customs yet, or had she given up? I only saw one of the kids put a finished assignment into a folder in her desk and take out a book.

I face my computer and open the multi-page form that I'll fill in and print out before tomorrow's meeting with Ms. Burnett. A committee of union-appointed teachers and district-appointed administrators wrangled over this form and procedure for several years. In the end, they decided that principals should judge merely Yes or No, good or bad, pass or fail for fifty-two "competencies."

"No" covers equally the abysmally incompetent, the burnt-out case who just goes through the motions, and the almost-there struggler who has cheerfully worked to master basics but has only managed four out of five. "Yes" covers all the territory between C-minus and superstardom. The reason for this exercise, say the state and the district, is "improvement of instruction." But it has neither a middle nor a high end, places along the learning curve that would allow us to chart progress.

To attain the summary rating "Meets the Standard" at the bottom of the form, a teacher has to be rated "Yes" on each and every competency, all fifty-two. Last week, for Mr. Ramirez, I lied a little. He is in his third year of teaching and I believe he'll be an outstanding teacher. On his form, I checked off an honest yes fifty-one times, and a dishonest yes on "Facilities are organized and maintained effectively to provide a clean, healthy, and safe environment."

In our meeting, I said, "Look at this first item under Environment. I didn't mark you down on it even though I could have."

He looked at it and then back at me, said, "Yeah, Sorry, I know it gets messy . . ."

I suggested that he set a time before lunch and at the end of the day for the kids to put things away and straighten the piles, to add Shelf Monitor to the classroom chore list. But I wouldn't use the evaluation form to show the absence of this one competency and didn't add the one drawback to the written record. I was unwilling to leave a capable teacher with a summary "Does Not Meet" just because he scores ninety-eight percent instead of a hundred!

But now, with my less able teacher, Ms. Burnett, I'll have to take that step. I'll probably spoil her day tomorrow. My sincere encouragement at the beginning and at the end of our meeting will only distract her briefly from the inevitable "Does Not Meet."

I have watched her fail to take a stand or to set limits when the fourth graders get rambunctious or bring a playground dispute in from recess. Just last week, in the changeover from reading period to math, I saw her consume—waste—ten minutes on something that should have taken two minutes at most. And she has not yet grown those eyes in the back of her head that every teacher must have. On visits to her classroom, I've watched entire dramas unfold just outside her field of view. Kids throw erasers and paper wads back and forth and crank pencils down to stubs in the old-fashioned sharpener and she doesn't notice.

But I'm not ready to give up on her. I won't compose such a bleak evaluation that she crashes, and I will not "counsel her out of teaching" by suggesting that she might better use her talents in another job. What other job? This is all she's ever wanted to do. Ms. Burnett got her degree and credential after ten years working as a library assistant. She loves kids, says she wants to improve her teaching, and asks for advice when she realizes something is not working. But past experience tells me that Ms. Burnett will be surprised when I mention the wrongly placed desks, the too-easy reading assignment, and the kids who didn't know what to do when they finished work.

Besides checking boxes, I also write comments under several headings. First I encourage: "Ms. Burnett has found some success in working with small groups to develop children's conceptual understandings of material introduced in whole-class lessons." But I can't leave it at that. "She also needs to develop and instill norms for large-group instruction that include turn-taking rather than free-for-all in discussion." I hesitate, deciding to tell Ms. Burnett in the conference rather than write on the form, that she needs to assert herself more as the adult-in-charge.

A totally honest appraisal would net her 15 or more marks of "No" on the checklist part of the form. Instead, I look for the three or four items that match my deepest concerns. I find four statements in the printed form, each written in educators' jargon. "The teacher monitors and continuously assesses student achievement for curricular planning and instructional improvement." Then, "Instructional time is used effectively." And two more. For all except these four, I check "Evident."

Because she will be a "Does Not Meet," I go on to write a required page that I'll clip to the rest of the pile. I offer a laundry list of suggestions for adding texture to the lessons. I give examples of more complex and interesting work she can assign to disorderly kids. And, I suspect for the hundredth time that the students' rowdy behavior is what they do to feel alive in a bland and boring classroom, but I'll bring this up carefully in our conversation and will not write a blunt statement about it.

Experienced at this, I manage to write the whole assessment and detailed suggestions in the thirty minutes I have allotted, even with two brief interruptions. In the first of these, I hand Benjy over to his father. In the second, I sign for a package delivered by the Airborne Express guy, who always manages to arrive just after the office staff has left. As I'm about to click Print for Ms. Burnett's evaluation, I pull the mouse pointer back. I decide to wait until morning in case I reconsider any of it during my 3:00 a.m. wake-and-worry.

2000, Brichta School

At the beginning of my last year, on the day after August registration, two women and a tiny girl stood in Brichta's front office. The tiny girl was Paula, a child with Down syndrome who'd turned five several months earlier. Paula's mother wanted Paula to attend regular kindergarten, and she'd brought an advocate with her to make this happen.

After years of carving out its own separate territory in school systems, whether by operating separate schools or separate classrooms within schools, special education was gradually changing its ways of doing business. At the same time, some families were hurrying these changes along without waiting for the system to catch up. Parents of many special needs children were now seeking inclusion of their children in regular classes instead of in the specialized classes and schools.

Just a couple of months earlier, Paula's mother had sat down with a team of professionals at another school and had agreed that Paula would join a class there, a class for other children with developmental delays. This class would have no more than twelve children and would be led by a teacher trained and certified to teach children with Down syndrome. At least one teacher assistant would further reduce the ratio of children to adults in the class, allowing more attention to each child. Now something had changed. Paula's mother wanted Paula in a regular kindergarten of more than twenty students with a teacher who had no assistant and who lacked training and experience in working with children with needs as special as Paula's.

The advocate recited the checklist of issues the school would be expected to address in Paula's classroom. The two that stood out for me were that Paula wore diapers and risked choking every time she put food into her mouth. My racing brain told me that the teacher could not leave the rest of the kids to diaper Paula and she could not diaper Paula off to one side while the other kids watched. I had no extra Somebody in any of our kindergarten rooms who could take care of Paula's diapers or supervise her eating. So I said "No. I can't register her until we get Paula's placement straightened out by central office."

The advocate protested for quite a while, but I stood my ground. She insisted that Paula's mother had the right to enroll Paula in her neighborhood school regardless of placement decisions made and agreed to earlier in the summer. I explained over and over that I could not guarantee Paula's safety with the staff I had now. After they left, I appealed to a specialist from downtown and repeated that I feared for Paula's safety unless she had one-to-one help in the classroom while we got her settled. Once again, I heard "Don't you have Somebody who . . . ?" Once again I wondered if any of the special education administrators had ever set foot in a school.

Pushing hard to make Paula's class placement and her safety my sole responsibility, central office set all the conditions, and insisted that I should come up, somehow, with the resources to carry out their orders. Even with the help of my supervisor, it took about six weeks to persuade the special education department to pay for an assistant to shepherd Paula in class for most of each day. I brought up the diapering issue with Karen, the health assistant.

"I can't ask her teacher to do the diapering in the classroom . . ."

"Tell the teacher to send Paula to me. One of the other kids can walk with her," Karen said. This was typical of Karen's unstinting generosity toward children and toward her colleagues.

When Paula started school, another advocate came to her classroom and led a discussion with the whole class. The woman said things like, "Paula loves pizza. How many of you love pizza?" About twenty minutes of this brought Paula a troop of five-year-old allies. If children from other classes bothered Paula on the playground or in the cafeteria, her classmates watched out for her and got the offender to leave her alone. Along with the rest of us, the other kids in Paula's class were thrilled for her when she moved from diapers to training pants sometime in late February. While we managed to reduce the amount of time Paula's aide spent with her, I had to beg for renewal of this temporary arrangement every six or eight weeks.

CHAPTER 19
TESTING

The Counselor

CONTRARY TO THE WISHFUL thinking of people in and outside of schools, a school counselor is not allowed to force her attentions on children who alarm us. More often than not, the parents of the alarming children already stand sideways to the system and refuse our interference. Our counselor's job was mainly to teach a district-created citizenship curriculum in the classrooms, and, in her spare time, to see some of the kids who disrupted or suffered.

By the district's rules of engagement and by her own training and experience, our counselor was not a therapist. So she listened, pacified, and contained. This grew more difficult each year as she worked to keep kids with mental disorders or dangerous behavior from causing harm to themselves or others. Even by my last year on the job, the district had never discussed the issue of children's mental health with its school leaders. Not once did they offer an orientation on this topic, preferring to view even psychotic manifestations through the narrow lens of "behavior."

The counselor, the teachers, and I could roughly divide troubled and troubling kids into the categories "needs discipline" or "needs counseling." Brichta's counselor and I never figured out a clear, once-and-for-all division of our work with troubled kids into counseling—her—and discipline—me. Because discipline and counseling touch or overlap at many points, we had to go case by case, event by event. The fact that she substituted for me when I left the building meant that sometimes she had no choice but to take over discipline. And every so often, I longed to be the good cop.

The fourth-grade boy I reported to the school security department during my last year on the job, the boy who drew pictures of guns and hypodermic needles, started acting up in third grade. When his teacher scolded him, Bradley launched into loud and disruptive denial, demanding that she "prove" he was the one who'd thrown the paper wad. By fourth grade, Bradley's smile grew more and more crooked and he exploded over small issues.

The counselor and I began to suspect an emotional condition that didn't leave him in control all the time. Bradley's mother had told us about her drug history and Bradley's father had told us about his mental illness, both supposedly cured by treatment. I suspected these revelations were meant to show us that they were people who *did something* about their problems. Even if they believed in some kind of cure for themselves, they wouldn't sign for Bradley to spend any time with our counselor.

Today, 4:45 p.m.

I pull the messy stack of today's mail and notes to the front and center of my desk. Four other piles sit nearby: the work to be done on the computer; the pile of things I need to do by next week (but might forget if I put them away); and, third, a couple of folders that need to go back into the filing cabinet. Last, the three-inch high stack of things to read when I have time sits in its permanent spot on the front left-hand corner of the desk. The items on the bottom have been there since September.

The first note in today's pile reminds me to nominate kids for camp scholarships. Every year, we get to send two names to the Y for their sleep-away camp. If we name the most needy children, their families often can't or don't answer phone calls, can't or won't pay attention to notes sent home, and don't get the children to the camp bus on time for departure. Then the scholarship goes unused.

We have to choose kids who might not need it *quite* as much but whose families face enough hardship to justify the free trip to camp. We need someone whose parents can receive and return phone calls, follow written instructions, and pull together as many items as they can from the *What-To-Take-To-Camp* list. I think of a brother and sister, aged eight and ten. Even though their mom was recently laid off from a low-wage job, she has a phone and a car, she comes to school, and she returns calls. I add a sticky note to the blank form.

> Yvonne,
>
> How about nominating Julia and Franco?
> I know Mikey needs it more, but I don't know
> if his grandma could manage the details.

2000–01, Brichta School

My next round of "no" is one that I'm more proud of than the one I gave to Paula's mother and her advocate, but perhaps I was enjoying the luxury of the lame duck. I had worked for at least one superintendent who expected that every child could score above average on the tests if we just taught them well enough. I never found out if he didn't grasp the mathematics of averages, or if he wanted to downplay means, medians, and standard deviations for reporters and politicians unfamiliar with this terrain.

Most holders of public office, plenty of journalists, and even a few of the principals I knew, couldn't have told you the difference between a raw score and a percentile rank. As a teaching assistant at Harvard and as a researcher in Tucson, I had learned enough about the science and craft of measurement to understand the tests' severe limitations. This knowledge left me anxious about misinterpretation by politicians and pundits.

If test results are poor or average or superior, *what happened* in the lives of children, both in and out of school, to produce—cause, engineer, evoke, provoke, beget—these particular outcomes? As my supervisors ramped up the talk about "results," the less they wanted to discuss *what we needed to do to get there*.

I believe that most of us who choose to be teachers or principals do so at least in part to serve our country by preparing children to function in community, to think, to earn a living, and to vote. When I started as a principal, we educators *did our best* to guide children to reach something we called *their highest potential*. I highlight the near-quaintness of this phrase because new vocabularies of economics, of promised punishments for imperfection, form a grim replacement.

During my time on the job, the definition of success itself shifted. We became less interested in pushing and inspiring each child do his or her best, and more engaged in the odd contortion of keeping everyone above average, as if that was statistically possible. In my school district, several new superintendents declared that we, the school district, would follow the core value that *every child can learn.*

Of course every child can learn. That's the North Star of education and should guide us in every part of the enterprise. In my district and in America, leaders got mixed up about this and fell prey to notions that every child could learn *the same things to the same levels,* and this became the new standard. Furthermore, we, the front-line educators, were failing if we did not produce this absurd hundred-percent result.

Most of my years at Brichta, the assistant superintendents entertained us with pep talks and handed over reams of test score data for us to analyze. They endorsed ideas like "School X put up motivational posters in the hallways and their scores went up last year!" and "School Y had an assembly—a rah-rah session—to pep up the kids to ace the tests, so it couldn't hurt to schedule one of those yourself." If anyone had bothered to look, they would have seen that, in the usual flow of such things, scores in these enthusiastic schools were up one year and down the next.

During my second-to-last year, I had the Brichta teachers meet in groups as well as individually with me to examine their kids' results from the year before, to analyze subtest weaknesses and strengths, and to concoct action plans for the year. At the end of that year, our scores were better than they'd been the previous year. That fall, at the beginning of my last year, I decided to scale back my approach. If Brichta's scores dropped, a possibility no matter what we did, it would give the principal who followed me a better chance to show good numbers at the end of her first year.

I gave each teacher two print-outs. First, I showed the results from his or her previous year's class along with school and district averages for the grade level. Second, I gave each a listing of how their current year's class had scored on the tests the previous year so they could see which of their children might need extra help. I reminded them that we were hearing a lot of chatter about test scores and teacher accountability. Then I shut up and didn't schedule any more meetings about the multiple-choice tests. That gave us time to explore the new writing assessments and the scoring rubrics and have some fun doing it.

I had something else in the back of my mind, too, something that fueled my anger about the process, but which even the "no" I said to singing and dancing our way to the tests could not affect: Once Down syndrome Paula or another equally delayed child was in third grade, the school would be required to test her in reading and math right along with other kids her age. Although Paula might take the tests separately from the class and have some questions read aloud to her, she'd face a pressure she'd not experienced before.

Furthermore, her scores would count in her school's overall performance ratings by state and federal agencies. I believe that this is wrong. But it's all part of the mythmaking, the notion that the ground is level and that outcomes relate only to the quality of teaching.

At both my schools, achievement scores were usually near district and state averages, sometimes a little above or a little below. When they were occasionally lower, they mirrored the economic make-up of my school communities. For the most part, children at both schools learned what they were supposed to learn. And some didn't, particularly the kids in the special needs classes, the kids in foster care, and the kids in chaotic and drug-endangered homes.

My research experience let me see exactly how the norm-referenced tests were a laughable measure of student learning. Do most people know that items on multiple-choice tests are not selected to assess a child's knowledge of the material? Instead, these questions have been identified in statistical trials as *likely to be missed by poorer-performing students and answered correctly by better-performing students regardless of knowledge of the content.* Test scores were never what woke me up in the middle of the night.

I refused to allow the curriculum in either of my schools to drill down on the tested subjects of language, reading, and math. Even though our state didn't test science, social studies, arts, and physical activity,

I insisted that teachers include these subjects in their weekly plans. As the climate in my school district grew more negative, I still had the autonomy, along with the support of the district's curriculum director, to steer teaching and learning in what I considered the right direction.

I loved our science curriculum during my last few years, but it did nothing to slow the tide of mentally ill and violent children, the threat of school shootings, the misuse of tests, or a new superintendent's set of show-off goals that sucked the morale right out of teachers and principals. I think back to the slogans, lists, mission statements, focus groups, orders both direct and unspoken, five-year-plans, fancy consultants, motivational speakers, organizational charts, military-sounding titles. Did any of these *help*? Some, yes, but most, no. Most of these messages remained off the point, a cover for how deeply misunderstood is the work in schools.

During my last couple of years, Brichta had a kindergarten teacher who'd transferred from a poverty-level inner city neighborhood. At her previous school, she'd taught first grade. One day in January of her first year, she remarked to me, "It took me a while to catch on, but I think my Brichta kindergartners come to school with the same level of skills as the first graders at my other school." Superintendents and school boards hesitate to acknowledge this discrepancy that comes from poverty and drug-afflicted families, or they deny that it exists because they don't want to come across as making excuses.

That last year, when I held no rallies, put up no posters, and didn't pressure the teachers, Brichta's scores improved, not just from the year before, but to the highest they'd been in three years. It would be magical thinking to suggest that reducing the pressure on the teachers is the answer all by itself, but that is no more magical an idea than the pep rallies, signs, and slogans.

CHAPTER 20
CRITICAL CARE

Families

ON THE DAY SHE ARRIVED at Brichta, Carol Ann wore a blue plaid dress and black patent Mary Janes with white lace socks, an outfit that might have been copied from a 1950s Norman Rockwell painting. She was eight years old, wore a plastered-on smile, and acted particularly eager to please her fostering relatives. I caught on very fast that Carol Ann's substitute parents intended to make up for *everything* Carol Ann had lost by being born to their son's ex-girlfriend.

Lots of children in foster care with family or strangers came to Brichta, as they had to Miller, and I have enormous regard for people who help raise children born to others. I have seen unintended hurt come to some of these children, children saddled with idealistic hopes and with the ego needs of their rescuers. In contrast to Steven's realistic grandparents, the older couple who'd taken in Carol Ann jacketed her tightly with their own ambition. While she was not the only child in this predicament, her pain remains the most vivid to me, as much for how she held it in as for how she acted it out.

While Mr. and Mrs. Woodard filled out the registration papers, Carol Ann sat in the upholstered chairs near the counter. After about five minutes, she got up to see what her guardians were doing. Then she perched again on the chair's edge so that her toes touched the floor. Most kids liked to lean back in that chair and swing their legs.

When I greeted her, Carol Ann spoke to me politely while she picked at a scab on her elbow, but her smile wavered. She told me that she was in second grade, but quickly added, "I should be in third." Mrs. Woodard told me that her husband's company had transferred him to Tucson.

Earlier, I had overheard the Woodards ask Mary, the registration clerk, to give Carol Ann a teacher who would make her "buckle down." This quaint phrase alerted me to the possibility that either we or Carol Ann faced some trials. Mary told the Woodards that Carol Ann would be in Mrs. Carlson's class, and at that point I joined their conversation because it was my job, not Mary's, to handle exceptions. Mrs.

Woodard repeated the "buckle down" business and I sidestepped, "Mrs. Carlson is an excellent teacher and I'm sure Carol Ann will like her a lot."

"But I want someone who'll be strict with her. Carol Ann doesn't need to *like* her."

I suggested that she set up a meeting with Mrs. Carlson and tell her about Carol Ann and find out about the curriculum. Glancing over at Carol Ann to let me know she had things to say outside of the child's hearing, Mrs. Woodard asked to talk with me in my office. She got to the point even before we sat down at the table: "That child can't read a word, and she's repeating second grade."

"Um-hmm," I nodded, waiting to hear more about what she wanted, which turned out to be a reading specialist, something we didn't have. I repeated the business about Mrs. Carlson being an excellent reading teacher, but Mrs. Woodard kept pressing me for testing, special reading help, a tutor, and more. As she left to walk with Carol Ann and Mary to Mrs. Carlson's room, I invited Mrs. Woodard to stay in touch.

Then I scribbled a note to the teacher.

> Check with me after school about your new student.

It turned out that we would be able to give Mrs. Woodard some of what she wanted, but not everything.

Over the next few weeks, her teacher found that Carol Ann could read a little, like a second-semester first grader. The retired teacher who volunteered to tutor Carol Ann confirmed the classroom teacher's impression: Carol Ann lacked confidence and stumbled badly when reading aloud from a familiar story. She was easily distracted.

Over my career, I ran into at least a dozen other families who expected the rescued child to make up all lost ground simply by virtue of the new family's good intentions and our best effort at school. Determined to redeem the sin of the vanished parent, these rescuers sometimes overwhelmed the child, right up to the brink of emotional abuse, with pressure to achieve, to succeed, to catch up in a magic moment. Some got defensive and angry when we asked about the child's early life. They would say, "That doesn't matter. He's with *me* now."

Too often, they did not just hope, but firmly expected, that taking this child into their lives would make up for prenatal drug exposure, malnutrition in early childhood, physical, sexual, or emotional abuse, family violence, or other trauma or deprivation. I also met fostering grandparents and determined adoptive parents who remained modest about raising a chosen or accidental child and who worked together with teachers, took the child to counseling, and provided loving support in all the right ways.

In the two years Carol Ann stayed at Brichta, her guardians grew increasingly hostile at our failure to bring Carol Ann "up to speed." Tests showed that Carol Ann was not learning disabled under district and state guidelines. Traditional IQ testing also revealed that, in that framework, Carol Ann's learning aptitude was in the low-average range. I worried most about how on-edge Carol Ann remained, how her little smile stayed rigidly in place even as tears of failure and frustration welled up when she couldn't do something.

I believed then, as I do now, that for kids born into poverty or abuse or haphazard homes, school *can* make kids smarter, can stretch their potential and strengthen their foundation. But I also knew then that school might never mend some of what troubled Carol Ann. She was born to a young drug-abusing mother. She was plucked from a chaotic family and household at the age of two and fostered at first by indifferent relatives. By the time she was three, Carol Ann's ability to reason and her sense of safety had already been damaged.

She was almost seven years old when the Woodards took her in and offered structure and ambition for the first time. Now we were supposed to erase Carol Ann's past in a few short months, to have her functioning at the level of her third-grade peers. Two years later, they relocated again when Mr. Woodard retired. From time to time I wonder if the Woodards ever smiled at Carol Ann or gave her a hug.

Today, 4:52 p.m.

A soft knock on the back door startles me just as I click to print Mr. McElroy's evaluation. Through the narrow window, I see Michele, an eighth grader I've known since she came to first grade at Miller during my last year there.

Michele's life story started out a lot like Jenifer's and like Carol Ann's, with drug-abusing and child-abusing parents, uncaring or unstable relatives, and foster care. But Michele had the good fortune to be adopted by her first-grade teacher. Opening the door, I see Michele's mom waiting in the car. Beginning the way she always does, Michele says, "Wanna know what I just did? I just finished reading the second Harry Potter book." Michele smiles with a silvery show of braces, and ducks her head a little, not completely trusting that I will grasp the importance of this. She knows that I know she has listened to the book's audio version already. Even so, reading it to herself is a big deal.

I say, "Wow! That's fantastic!" and I give her a sideways hug before she heads back out to the car. Her mom and I wave at each other, and they take off.

I wonder what Jenifer's life will be when she is Michele's age. The efforts of child welfare to reassemble Jenifer's family have given her enough false hope to last two lifetimes. Mom has abandoned drug rehab five or six times and makes it to one scheduled visit out of four. Jenifer, though, has not stopped believing that the big reunion might happen tomorrow.

1999–2000, Brichta School

When I was in the sixth grade, my friend Linda's class-mate Penny died suddenly at the end of an otherwise normal Thursday at school. There was talk that a softball had hit her in the head during a playground game. That was the first time I ever heard of a child getting killed by something that happened at school, but I can still remember Linda's mother calling my mother that night, and then the front-page article in the next day's newspaper, with the photo of a girl I had once met at a birthday party.

In an America where everything was possible, even after the Columbine school massacre and before Newtown, we—public education—along with the public itself, were hostage to the notion that we could keep all the kids safe if we only tried hard enough. It would be our fault—the school's fault, not the fault of the Evil Unknown—if we failed.

Central office expected everyone to play along with this illusion not only of control, but also of responsibil-ity. One day, probably in the fall of 1999, the district ordered every principal to assemble a committee and draft an emergency plan. In Brichta's plan, we addressed every issue listed in the district's disaster guide, regardless of how unlikely its occurrence. Then we trained staff and informed parents. Every time the district sent representatives to a FEMA training, they brought back new guidelines and rules, sometimes ones that contradicted the previous batch.

We practiced evacuation, lockdown, and accounting for every person on our campus. Never mind that a determined shooter would be able to see any spot in a classroom through the big windows Tucson put into its 1950s schoolhouses. When I asked about buying and storing required emergency supplies, like water, food, blankets, first aid kits, and flashlights, the school district's response was, "Hmmm. I guess you could ask your PTO."

When, months later, I finally received feedback on our 20-page preparedness plan, it was criticized for being "too detailed." So I boiled it down to a couple of pages supplemented by maps and charts, and sent it in again. Nothing more was said until the following year, when we were told to create "more detailed plans." I pulled the old "too detailed" plan out of my computer and sent it in. It was received with no further comment.

No one ever came back from a FEMA training to suggest what elementary schools are best equipped to do, to build social and emotional bridges, to bolster community. The kids who shot up a Colorado high school were its own students, just showing up as usual that morning. We could not, then or now, distinguish swashbuckling from this-might-be-the-big-one. I felt frightened for us, for my own lack of confidence in facing down an armed assailant.

Columbine did not make me fear external danger more than before, but the discussion got tricky. Even after Newtown, these tragedies will remain horrific rare occurrences. At the same time, the emotional potency of such a catastrophe takes a kind of precedence over the logical, the possible, or the likely. Our fear will run right past the fact that there was an armed police officer at Columbine, that the school in Newtown had a locked entrance, that the killer's weapons were legally obtained.

Whenever someone who has been a student—and who hasn't been?—commits a terrible crime, the media turn to the school for answers. Didn't you see it coming? Didn't you try to do something about it?

Yes, for God's sake, we did see it coming. We did try to do something. But no one we told took us seriously, or felt that it was quite their place to do something, or was willing to take on the angry and defensive parents of the child-suspect. When the parents protested that little Robert or Jeffrey or Oscar couldn't possibly, was only playing, didn't mean it, the district preferred that I just be nice.

On the other hand, how can you know who is a menace? At least three of my former students have been charged with murder. Even the daydreaming nine-year-old who evolved into the 20-year-old schizophrenic who killed two family members did not wear a sign on his forehead when I knew him at Brichta. In the years that followed, did his high school teachers raise an alarm over something we didn't see in elementary school, or was he just another moody teenager?

I didn't spend much time worrying that a mass murderer would pin down or mow down our campus. But I wondered if my turn would come to have a child, like Linda's friend Penny, seriously injured or killed at school while playing, fighting, stepping on a rattlesnake, or skateboarding on the roof.

Today, 4:55 p.m.

In the blue folder that holds my opened-and-sorted U.S. mail, I find a letter from the state welfare department asking about the special needs category of one of our kids. Once a year or so, I get these letters when a parent applies for Social Security based on a child's disability. I set it on a pile for tomorrow. In the yellow folder that holds my district mail, the first item is a bad photocopy of a state law that was passed last year, with no explanation of why I'm getting it now.

Some items from each folder go directly into the trash. These include a 5" by 8" postcard in three colors from the superintendent's office reminding me about a meeting that is already on my calendar; an offer for six-dollar tickets to a musical performance we do not have in our budget; a membership form from a professional organization I have joined and left many times because I can never find time to read their magazine; and, finally, an invitation to a luncheon honoring a retired educator I admire, but set for a weekday when I can't possibly get away.

Last, I toss out a brochure that offers, for only $99, a workshop that promises to reveal the secret of controlling aggressive and violent children. Susie knows how to get rid of most of these before I see them, but she still leaves one or two that she knows will make me laugh.

In my email, I find a reply from our central-office risk and safety specialist. About a month ago, twelve-inch acoustic tiles started falling from the ceiling of a second grade classroom. I asked the school district maintenance department for help, but they assigned it a low priority for repair. Yesterday, seeking leverage, I sent a copy of the message to the safety manager. Now he suggests that we either move the second grade class out of its room until all the ceiling tiles can be secured or have the custodian "try to figure something out."

I reply:

Matt,

We have no extra rooms here. There's no way not to occupy a second grade classroom! I'll have the custodians go after the tiles with a broom handle to knock all the loose ones down while the kids aren't there.

Thanks,

Caroline

In the next fifteen minutes I draft: (1) a stern form letter to parents of frequently tardy or absent children so that Mary can personalize these and send them out; (2) a note to the afternoon custodian asking him to stop by so we can talk about Patrick earning time to tag along with him; (3) a memo to first- and second-grade teachers reminding them to attend an information session about the new reading books they'll start using next year; and (4) a repeat memo to staff to keep track of personal medications, since I've found an estrogen tablet on the floor of the women's restroom for the second time.

As has become my habit for the past two years, I check online news to make sure nothing really bad has happened since morning.

Chapter 21
Are You Busy?

Today, 5:15 p.m.

JASON, THE YOUNG afternoon custodian, appears in my doorway to tell me that a woman is letting her big white dog run around on our soccer field. The faded "No Dogs Allowed" signs that hang from our chain link fence have never quite accomplished their purpose. Nearly every day, the new houses south and west of the schoolyard send dogs and their people to our grassy field. Trying to reduce encounters between children and dog poop, I've asked Jason to tattle on the dog-runners when he sees them out there.

Now, I've got to go out to the field and present myself as the principal who doesn't want dog doo tracked into the building. I doubt that any of our visiting dog lovers can imagine the custodian carrying a nine-by-twelve rug out of a kindergarten room mid-morning because of what one child has brought inside on their sneakers. I make sure I have my keys and hurry out the back door.

The woman doesn't look up until I'm almost there. She glances at me before turning back to watch the white dog as it races toward her, tongue lolling, doggy-smiling. She carries nothing for cleaning up the dog's leavings. Wanting to act cordial even with an unwelcome visitor, I still use a loud "hello" to get her to pay attention, to acknowledge my presence. I make sure to pronounce the word *principal* clearly even though this is not our first encounter over the white dog. She looks toward me again, but does not make eye contact.

"Sorry," I say, "We don't allow dogs. The kids step in the poop and track it inside." I wish I had just gone ahead and said "shit." When you're cleaning it off of little kids' shoes, that's what it is.

She doesn't say anything at all while she re-attaches the dog's leash. I suspect she knows and doesn't care that it has already done its business somewhere out on the field. Her silence seems more belligerent than embarrassed, so I figure she'll start bringing her dog later in the day, when the cars are gone from the parking lot. I stand there in the shadows of the March afternoon until the two of them reach the opening in the fence and make their way down the slope that separates Brichta's playground from the street.

Walking back, I spot a boy riding a bicycle in the parking lot. Closer, I see that the rider is Steven from Mr. McElroy's class. This isn't the first time Steven has ridden back to school in the late afternoon. His city-required helmet dangles by its strap from the bike's handlebars.

Only four or five cars remain in the lot, and it's not likely that one of them will back out and hit him. But I live in the liability shadow, so I hurry toward him. Steven sees me and speeds right up to where I stand. Does he think I'm going to announce that the rules have changed? Since I've recited the no-riding rule to Steven every couple of weeks for the past two years, a scolding will offer him no new information, but that doesn't stop me.

"Steven," I start. "You know you're not supposed to be riding your bike here."

"My Tata says I can ride my bike to school."

He is playing with that ambiguous parent permission that some kids think tops school rules and principal's orders. This collection of overgeneralized permissions includes "My dad said to defend myself if someone bothers me," and "My mom said I could go to my friend's house after school."

"Sorry, kiddo," I say to Steven. "We've been through this before. You can't ride your bike through the parking lot no matter what your Tata says."

Steven runs through three or four facial expressions, shrugs, then says a cheerful "OK." He jumps on to the bike, and rides fast through the parking lot and out into the street.

Sheets of Paper

I have never been someone who listed pros and cons before making important decisions. Instead, I just made

the decision, just *walked through the door in front of me.*
This is how I departed from the principalship. One day
I noticed that I would feel better walking through the
door marked "EXIT" than I would feel not walking
through it. Just as I entered the profession on a dare
and something of a whim, not analyzing or plotting my
decision, I began the process of separation. I had until
January to make it official, but once I started telling
people in September that it would be my last year, I
kept walking.

When my high school friend had posed the question about the sheet of paper eventually crushing you,
my mind rejected this query altogether, but in later
years it crept up on me. What are the things that in
a single instance barely catch your attention, but in
the accumulation of mass or time, can crush you? For
me, it was never the paper, either a single sheet or
the piles on my desk.

At any particular moment, I might be dealing simultaneously with seriously troubled kids, an incompetent
employee, a teacher's long-term illness, a cafeteria
worker vacancy, someone's divorce, a school board
member's whims, and a major remodel of our school
building. An educator arrives on the job knowing that
we must not only foster the learning of the whole
flock, but also do our best to repair, even rescue,
individual children who live at risk. Sometimes I wondered if it had been a mistake altogether to bring my

catalogue-librarian personality to a job that demanded social skills, multi-tasking, strong emotional intelligence, and the ability to remain unruffled under pressure.

Is it the job of a public elementary school—as currently organized and funded—to compensate for every medical, emotional, social, and other trauma a child might have faced? In real life, most educators I know find themselves genuinely committed to this ideal. We worry deeply about a child who is troubled or who fails to learn, and we search for all available help. I was diligent, attentive to doing right, yet still reached the ends of my time, my ability to manage the all-at-onceness of it, my capacity for sadness, and, sometimes, my wits.

Of a calendar year's 8,760 hours, kids spend only about 1,100 of those in school. This amounts to about twelve percent of their young lives. Exactly how are we supposed to make up for what goes on during the hours they are elsewhere, in other hands, to fix what even a functioning family can't always manage?

What did I fear and where did my courage fail? I never stopped worrying that a child in my charge would die. I'd known such a thing was possible, ever since a girl I'd once met died at school when we were both kids. Several principals I knew had had students die at school, the tragedy of the death compounded by years of traumatic lawsuits. Then came Columbine, and my anxiety grew.

When did my energy for the accumulated burden just give out without my noticing the moment it happened? Was it *one more thing*, a final straw that was identifiable, quantifiable, or preventable?

When school began in August of my seventh year at Brichta, I told the teachers that we had one more year together. I said that I didn't plan to be a lame duck, whatever that was, and we'd keep on doing the right thing for kids, whatever that was.

Not long after that, a teacher stopped me in the hallway before school one morning and asked me if I had a minute to talk. "I hate to ask you for this," she said. "It's the kind of thing you always say 'no' to."

She wanted to take her fifth graders to an archeological dig about an hour's bus ride from school. The district only had budget for closer-to-home trips that took a half-day. Even though Margo had already found a generous friend to pay for the extra fuel and the bus driver's time, I'd have to make calls and get papers signed to cover the special permissions we needed.

My stomach clenched and my neck prickled. I do not remember what Margo and I said to conclude the conversation. I might have said "yes," but I'm just as likely to have stammered and hedged and said I would "try." I retreated to my office and closed the door for a while, something I almost never did.

My job—the ordinary and the extraordinary, the routine and the save-the-day—was outrunning me.

I was already planning to leave, finish, retire at the end of the year, but I hadn't realized that my growing resistance to the job was jeopardizing the very thing I'd come here to do. What was I here for, if not to help teachers navigate the system so they could do the most important job in the world—teach kids?

I still do not think I was completely burned out. When something offered refreshment and renewal along with the extra work, I often did seize the opportunity. During my last three years, I had some of the best times of my career with a science program created for the school district by some plucky high school teachers who had won a big grant. Kids observed, counted, documented, described, diagrammed, inquired further, and reported their experiences handling animal, vegetable, and mineral materials. The complex curriculum lined up with my values for learning as much as anything I've done as an educator.

But the science program could not keep things like *this* from happening: I slept poorly for weeks when a father threatened to kidnap his fifth-grade daughter from school when he was released from prison the following month. This child's class was in one of the portables. The person I spoke with at School Security just said to keep the door locked, and so we did. It took three weeks to determine that the convict-father had gone to Mexico and was unlikely to return. Meanwhile, the class suffered a hundred interruptions each day as kids left for bathrooms inside the main building, then knocked on the door to get back into their portable. A determined kidnapper could have stood around the corner and waited until one of these restroom trips to let himself in.

Today, 5:30 p.m.

Back at my desk, I find the note I wrote this morning about the woodpecker hole in Mr. McElroy's portable. Since I have forgotten all day to ask Susie to send in a repair order, I spend two minutes writing an email to Maintenance. I remember to add a copy for Susie before I hit send.

Just as I finish checking the news on my computer, a second-grade teacher appears in my doorway. She stays late like this at least a couple times a week. "Are you busy?" she says. Everyone knows I'm *never* not busy, that the question means, "Are you too busy for us to talk right now?"

"Come on in," I say. She perches on the edge of one of the blue chairs, takes a deep breath, and says, "Um, I'm applying for the Master's program in library science. Can you write me a reference letter?"

She sees the look of disappointment and alarm on my face, so I quickly reassure her that my consternation is over the prospect of losing her. She's a talented teacher and will make a wonderful librarian. But I hate it each time an excellent teacher decides to go for a specialty job outside the classroom, whether it's librarian, counselor, or instructional coach. Those are important jobs too, and I want them filled with capable people, but each time one of my classroom treasures makes the leap, it is a loss. Once we agree that early next week is soon enough for the reference letter, she leaves and I sit back in my chair and roll my head around to relax my neck.

Still hoping to be on time for my 6:00 p.m. board meeting at the Y, I pick up the phone and make my second attempt to reach Ricky's dad. When I tried an hour ago, Ricky answered the phone and said his dad was in the shower. This time, Ricky's seventh-grade brother answers. When I ask to speak to his dad, the brother booms out, "*Da*-ad, it's Dr. *Tomp*-kins."

I hear Ricky in the background. "Ooops, I forgot to tell you."

Ricky's dad gets on the line with a curt "'lo."

I tell him that Ricky caused trouble on the bus this morning and that I'm waiting for a ticket from the driver. I say that Ricky might get kicked off the bus for a few days, and that he stayed extra wound up even after Karen gave him his pill. Trying to put a positive tone into my voice, I add that Ricky didn't get into a fight today even though there was talk of one. When I pause, Ricky's dad just says, "OK. Thanks."

We are off the phone in a few more seconds, no mention of Marcia or any big changes for the family. If the parent had been Ricky's mother, and not his silent dad, I think I might have said something, at least would have suggested letting Ricky's teacher know that Marcia had left.

On this late winter day of my final year at Brichta, my final year as principal, I have made progress with the stacks of paper on my desk, but I sense that they have gained on me since morning. I didn't start pulling the assault referrals out of the pile next to the computer. I only found an awkward and time-consuming fix for the hole in our substitute teacher budget. I did not get back to the mom about the new shirt I refuse to provide for her son. I didn't write up the agenda for tomorrow's faculty meeting. Even though I've seen him two or three times since the child study meeting, I forgot to ask the afternoon custodian if he'd help out with Patrick's behavior reward.

Some of the other Did Nots aren't so bad. Caleb and Mitchell did not fight, nor did Ricky. The boys in Ms. Langer's special education class made it through the day despite their reasons why not. Down syndrome kindergartner Paula stayed dry and didn't choke on her lunch.

Ed Bell, the Man in the Principal's Office, might not recognize this March Tuesday as a possible day in the life. But I'm satisfied with today. I have persevered, have juggled the unexpected with the scheduled, and have spent time with kids and teachers and other staff for whom I care deeply. I have made choices and decisions consciously and conscientiously, have accomplished familiar tasks proficiently and have responded successfully to surprises.

Rushing now to be only a couple of minutes late, I check my wire basket for any last-minute notes and, finding none, I close the door between my office and the darkened reception area. I pull my purse out of the file drawer and transfer car keys to my hand, then tuck the pouch with my school keys into the nylon briefcase.

Only after I have allowed the back door to close and lock behind me do I notice a crumpled sheaf of first-grade worksheets lying on the sidewalk, dropped and forgotten by their owner. I work my way into the briefcase and pull out the keys, unlock the door, and pitch the papers in the direction of my round table. When they land on the floor instead, I do not walk inside to pick them up.

AFTER

DAVE WAS RIGHT. Most of the time, in both my schools, I had the freedom and the authority to decide what would happen—what we *did*. As a principal, I got to say, suggest, encourage, push, demand, and, I hope, inspire and provoke a great deal of what went on in classrooms and in the school as a whole. I started the job at a time when my school district still welcomed creative and diverse school leaders. They had space for teddy bears, curmudgeons, and even for eggheads.

Staying true to my vision, I succeeded in generating and sustaining collaborative work. I learned not only to work with teachers and staff, but to bring both my mind and heart to my work with children and their families. I learned to deal with high-stakes challenges that came out of nowhere, that forced me to learn something new in the moment. At the same time, I was rarely mentored and was expected to function independently, even as a beginner with no experience. The fair measure of autonomy I enjoyed on the job operated as the twin of professional loneliness.

Both Miller and Brichta were, in the scheme of things, easy schools filled with adults and children I cared about. *School*, in the abstract and the concrete, remains my natural habitat. But my fifteen-year run on the job brought me to believe that the job of principal has become precariously misshapen and that the larger institution of public education has failed to address this.

It's not difficult to see how the quantity of work has mushroomed. The less obvious piece is the precipitous increase in the *stakes*, the threats and dangers, and the collateral anxiety generated by some altogether new tasks. Two aspects of this growth are highly visible, while two others remain hidden from general notice.

First, and with good reason, we are engaged in a frantic effort to close the achievement gap between rich and poor. *This takes a lot of time.* I don't mean just the years invested in a national effort, but hours of a principal's work week. To boost student learning, school systems target teacher quality through on-the-job classes that are provided or attended by the principal. Today's necessary spotlight on teacher excellence has generated more complex procedures for evaluating how they do their jobs. As the leader of instruction, the principal coordinates and conducts these time-consuming performance appraisals, after which she provides meaningful feedback and supportive supervision. This is not a mechanizable part of running a school.

Second, the moment-to-moment attention to student safety that school leaders must pay has ratcheted up the anxiety level, the psychic load, of the work. Columbine took us from a rather easygoing faith-based approach to a yellow-alert array of responses in which careful planning would save us. Newtown raised this level at least to orange and further reduced our confidence that we could prevent disaster no matter how carefully we anticipated the possibilities.

The job description hardly ever mentions two less-visible areas of both workload and worry-load. First, we live with a systemic ambivalence over inclusion or separation, not to mention supervision, of children with severe and complex mental health or learning needs. The situations must be managed case by case. Hours of sitting in highly emotional meetings is just one feature of this. I believe that by my final year at Brichta, I was spending twenty percent—one day in five—of my work week taking care of half a dozen extreme-need children. It was no one else's job to care for the kids who spun out of control.

The other big item that gets left off the job description is the constant and necessary attention to legal procedures, to due process, to teachers' union contracts, and to avoiding lawsuits. Like any responsibility that rests on dodging trouble, rather than on creating and producing, the costs in anxiety and worry can be high.

Now, years into retirement, I pay attention to various American initiatives to improve the quality of principals without addressing the content of the work that these better principals will do. These twenty-first century principals will have knowledge and skills that far surpass mine; these better principals will work both harder and smarter; they will *do more*. Rarely do these reform schemes mention who will take time with the children now that the principal is an engineer. And even more rarely do they mention the possibility of drastically restructuring the principal's actual work.

In the last years of the twentieth century, I watched American public education leave its foundation in *accomplishment* and move over to embrace *punishment*. Accountability has come to stand for the penalties that will be applied to students, teachers, and principals who do not meet very narrowly defined targets. It is difficult to celebrate accomplishment when you are working as hard as you can to avoid punishment.

I still do not believe our work is futile, but that it is *wrongly imagined*. I continue to label myself a cranky optimist, someone who thinks we *can* have schools where children learn and where adults can enjoy their work. My inner optimist dreams that there is still a chance for public schools to be the one civic institution—the common ground—where we practice being citizens, in it together.

ENDNOTES

1   James Herndon, *How to Survive in Your Native Land* (New York: Bantam Books, 1972), page 10. Along with works by Jonathan Kozol, this was among the first of the "radical" school reform books I read while I was preparing to be a teacher and during my first few years on the job.

2   Little, J.W., "Norms of Collegiality and Experimentation: Workplace Conditions of School Success." American Educational Research Journal, 1982. Vol. 19, No. 3, pages 325–340.

3   Harry F. Wolcott, *The Man in the Principal's Office* (Prospect Heights, IL: Waveland Press, Inc., 1984; reissue of original work published by the University of Oregon in 1973). Wolcott's ethnographic study was conducted in 1966 and 1967, and is regarded as a "classic" in the study of educational leadership.

4   Researcher Nan Stein of the Wellesley College Centers for Women published her first scholarly article on sexual harassment among schoolchildren in 1987. It was not until 1991 that word of this phenomenon started reaching a wider public. I recall first reading reports

of the Stein research in newspapers in 1992. A useful early article is found in the archive of *The New York Times,* June 10, 1993, "Fighting Sexual Harassment in the Schools," by Carin Rubenstein.

[5]   A 1992 US Supreme Court decision, *Franklin vs. Gwinnett County Public Schools* affirmed the right of families to sue school districts for damages when the school failed to take action to intervene in sexual harassment that resulted in harm to the student. This suit was first filed in the Georgia courts in 1988 and was decided nearly two years before the equity officer for my school district said he did not know what I was talking about when I reported the chest-touching incident at Miller.

Acknowledgments

W HETHER SHE KNOWS IT or not, Kathy Kimball got this whole thing started by appearing on National Public Radio to discuss the challenges facing principals. Our subsequent email correspondence planted the seeds of this book.

My longest-time friend Linda Elliott Polito asked a key question as the book was getting underway and, whether she knew it or not, she rode on my shoulder throughout its writing and re-writing. Also vital to this process has been Linda's husband Sam L. Polito, who not only recruited me to work in public schools, but remained unflagging in his support and cheerleading.

I am deeply grateful to Lindley Hunter Silverman for her friendship and coaching as I tried to turn myself into a writer of memoir.

Melody Webb and Robert Utley, writers and dear friends, gave me some useful craft suggestions and have kept up their encouragement over the span of the project.

As a workshop junkie, I have shared drafts of this work with so very many people it would be impossible to name everyone who made a helpful suggestion. The writing teachers and workshop colleagues who've helped move my work along include Gregory Martin at two Taos summer workshops; Jennifer Brice at two Colgate summer workshops; and my colleagues at the two Gribner workshops, particularly Michael Carman, Ron Grant, and the late Susan Ribner.

I also deeply appreciate the responses to earlier versions of my full-length manuscript provided by Jennifer Simpson, Susan Gibbs, and Cynthia Patton. Lawrence Hippler had helpful suggestions for specific sections of the final draft. Toward the end, I have benefited greatly from the help of Ladette Randolph and Jane von Mehren, and from my fellow writers in Jane's 2014 Taos workshop.

During the entire time I was writing this book, teacher colleagues Barbara Hawk and Maryann Nuckolls let me pester them with questions about our work together. They helped me remember who I was at the beginning, middle, and end of my career as principal. Jane Fitzgerald corroborated a crucial detail. Teachers and district staff who responded to specific questions included Fran Braverman, Gloria Carrington, Sheralyn Gray, Gail Hall, Nancy Mueller, Alma Robles, Betty Sanchez, and Pam Stein. My friend and colleague Myna Matlin read an early draft and gave me useful feedback.

Entomologists John Edwards and Justin Schmidt helped me get my Africanized bee details in order.

Seymour Sarason did not live to see the results of his suggestion that I write about what it was like to move from one school to another. That early piece of sage advice bore far more fruit than I expected when I first heard it.

I send a thousand thanks to the three individuals without whom I would not have become a principal when I did: David Kennon, who dared me; Eugene Benton, who hired me and supervised me kindly and wisely for all my years at Miller School; and Raúl Grijalva, who had faith that I could work in a multicultural school.

I send out a big hug to my former student who showed up as Ricky. I think he knows that I'll love him forever and that I'm thrilled that he has reconnected with his mother.

From here, it gets tricky, because literally hundreds of people enriched the life and career that I have explored in this book. These unwitting assistants include students, teachers, non-teaching school staff, district administrators, parents, my colleagues, and the wonderful women who ran the front offices of my schools and the ones who transcended the bureaucracy in central office.

And Mom, Miri, Tom, and Cindy—thanks for knowing I could do it and treating it like a real book all along. Dad, you didn't see this one finished, but you always believed I could do it. I love you all!

Author Contact: Caroline@sunflowerlexical.com
Permissions: Permissions@sunflowerlexical.com
Website: sunflowerlexical.com.
Facebook: PrincipalTheBook
Blog: http://principalthebook.blogspot.com/

CPSIA information can be obtained at www.ICGtesting.com
Printed in the USA
LVOW06s1552270815

451790LV00001B/113/P